I0074630

BLESSED STRATEGY

A SPIRITUALLY-BASED GUIDE
for Growing Your Business
and Leading with Purpose

DR. GEORGE TAYLOR III

Copyright © 2019 Dr. George N Taylor III/EntOrgCorp LLC.

All rights reserved. No part of this book may be reproduced, stored, or transmitted by any means—whether auditory, graphic, mechanical, or electronic—without written permission of the author, except in the case of brief excerpts used in critical articles and reviews. Unauthorized reproduction of any part of this work is illegal and is punishable by law.

This book is a work of non-fiction. Unless otherwise noted, the author and the publisher make no explicit guarantees as to the accuracy of the information contained in this book and in some cases, names of people and places have been altered to protect their privacy.

Scripture quotations taken from the King James Version of the Bible.

Scripture quotations taken from the New American Standard Bible® (NASB),
Copyright © 1960, 1962, 1963, 1968, 1971, 1972, 1973,
1975, 1977, 1995 by The Lockman Foundation
Used by permission. www.Lockman.org

ISBN: 978-0-578-22203-5 (sc)
ISBN: 978-0-5782-2227-1 (e)

Because of the dynamic nature of the Internet, any web addresses or links contained in this book may have changed since publication and may no longer be valid. The views expressed in this work are solely those of the author and do not necessarily reflect the views of the publisher, and the publisher hereby disclaims any responsibility for them.

Any people depicted in stock imagery provided by Getty Images are models, and such images are being used for illustrative purposes only. Certain stock imagery © Getty Images.

Dr. George Taylor III/EntOrgCorp LLC
1779 Kirby Parkway, 1-41 Germantown, TN 38138
901-240-2058

Lulu Publishing Services rev. date: 08/27/2019

DEDICATION

I dedicate this book to God, my wife, my mother,
and to the memory of my beloved dad.

CONTENTS

INTRODUCTION

Throughout my time as a business professional, entrepreneur, consultant, professor, and researcher, I have focused intently on solving problems. For example, as the owner of an organizational development consulting firm, I focus on addressing three areas articulated by organizational leaders: organizational strategy mapping and alignment; leveraging capabilities of people, processes, and systems; and, maximizing utility of resources. As a professor, I work to resolve instances of knowledge gaps and facilitate learning processes so that students are equipped with the skills and provided information they need to achieve their purpose. As a researcher and business consultant, I provide solutions to business problems that impact the growth and survivability of business firms.

The needs mentioned above are often big problems and helping to solve these problems has brought many of my clients and students, success, and for me, a great deal of professional and personal satisfaction. Yet, in working to solve these problems over the last few years, I too have also learned. I learned a great deal about myself and the nature of others. I have had the honor and opportunity to work with some of the brightest minds one can expect to encounter. And, through these encounters, I have nourished my true spiritual self.

Although it's not always explicitly stated, the majority of business leaders and managers across the industries and sectors that I have come in contact with are often grounded by a spiritual force. And, when I investigate the business principles and philosophies that guide these leaders, I receive comments that sound like this: "We are committed to doing good things." Or, "Our purpose is to connect with others and demonstrate that much good comes from doing good." The underlying themes of these discussions are based upon spiritual principles. This is good news yet also cause for some concern. The good news is that these business owners and professionals recognize that businesses should serve a purpose; a purpose that includes profit, for sure, yet also extends beyond profit. A purpose that seeks to connect the business to its customers, community, and the larger society. The drawback is that there remains a belief that the explicit articulation of being a spiritually-based leader or having a spiritually-based business is something to shun or that reference to biblical (or belief equivalent) principles somehow makes the company weak. There may also be a belief that such spiritually-based connections and principles make it seem that the company is simply riding the wave of spiritual sentiment, making such efforts unauthentic or faddish. At the other end of the spectrum, and related to this notion, is that a spiritually-based purpose and culture is bad for business. That it represents a push toward unwanted belief systems and principles in a world where the business should appear as a secular artifact within a contemporary landscape. Scharmer, a protégé and colleague of Peter Senge, writes, "Is the rise of spirituality just an epiphenomenon of the baby-boom generation's growing more reflective, or is it related to a cultural shift in society at large?[1]"

As I prepared to write this book, I thought deeply about what it means to be a spiritually-based business leader and entrepreneur. I reflected on the business leaders that I truly thought were effective from a spiritually-based perspective. I researched and spoke with business leaders that truly motivate their employees and engage their customers. I reflected upon leaders with reputations of not only being astute business entrepreneurs and business leaders, but also have strong community reputations that represented spiritually-based principles. I spoke with and researched entrepreneurs and organizational leaders that represented courage and "did not hide in the tall grass," making their spiritually-based belief systems known.

In reflecting on spiritually-based business leaders, I not only reflected upon the traits, I dug deep into the performance actions and results of these leaders. I immersed myself in literature and spent hundreds of hours

---

[1] "Learning from the Future as It Emerges." 2009, p. 92. *Theory U.*

reviewing my interviews and journals. A few consistent themes continually reappeared during my inquiry and reflections:

- Spiritually-based entrepreneurs and leaders build long-lasting cultures. While writing this Introduction, the founder of Chick-fil-A, S. Truett Cathy had recently died at the age of 93. A glance at the headlines read *Chick-fil-A Founder Credited His Success to Christian Principles* (NPR, 2014, September 8) or Rick Warren's opinion that *Chick-fil-A Founder Truett Cathy Truly Lived His Faith* (Time, 2014, September 9). The culture of Chick-fil-A remains one of the most admired cultures, and although there are critics, the company is clear in its values and be rest assured that the culture built by Cathy will remain for quite some time.
- Spiritually-based entrepreneurs and leaders, and their organizations, show a sincere, deep concern for their customers, value-chain partners, and employees. Howard Schultz, former CEO and Chairman of Starbucks, is perhaps one of the most well-known examples of this. In fact, one can reflect back during the economic crisis of 2007-2008 and recall how many customers and business observers claimed that Starbucks had lost its way. That the focus on the customer and the experience – the elements that made the company truly unique – got lost during the leadership "churn" the chain experienced during the early 2000s. In comes Schultz, who refocused the Starbucks back to its roots – its culture - to regain its market position and presence. In fact, I wrote this chapter in a Starbucks location where a manager was interviewing applicants. Although I do not agree with open-store interviews, one statement really stood out to me: the manager, in telling his story, remarked that "I fell *in love* with the company."
- Spiritually-based entrepreneurs and leaders, and their organizations build a connection with their communities and target specific areas of concern. A well-known example of this is ServiceMaster, a company that serves commercial and residential customers by providing a vast array of maintenance offerings ranging from pest control, lawn care, and other landscaping needs. What makes this company special is that its spiritual values are tied to concrete

business goals, which include having a strong commitment to its local community and society at large.

These themes were not only interesting, they were astounding. These are the principles, traits, and performance standards that are indicative and associated with high-performance organizations. In plain language, the behaviors related to spiritual leaders correlate with the performance principles that matter.

From an entrepreneurial and business researcher perspective, I believe that individuals that start businesses are instrumental to the health of the national and international economies. It is the entrepreneur that scales her business, which provides jobs that grow economies, markets, and industries. With that belief, coupled with my own extensive history and experience as an entrepreneur, I wanted to provide a guide for entrepreneurs and small business owners to gain the benefit of a framework that focuses on long-term strategic success. Yet, I thought it was important to do this from a spiritually-based perspective.

Make no mistakes, there is no shortage of books that outline the steps to strategy planning and execution; however, there is a need for a business guide with a practical focus on strategy planning and execution for entrepreneurs, leaders, and companies that have a goal of operating from a spiritually-based perspective. There is a need for a comprehensive framework that helps entrepreneurs and small business owners embed spiritual approaches into their company's DNA; its culture, from the beginning.

The content and layout of this book is designed to have you not only rethink your business yet also to encourage you to reflect upon your individual and business purpose. It's designed to get you and your team to go beyond schematic changes and encourage ways to ensure that your business approach is indeed spiritually-based from the beginning, and that your approach is authentic and consistent with who you are.

Next, this book is comprehensive, and while there are some common themes of strategy planning and execution, there are plenty of fresh perspectives. These perspectives are based on spiritual and biblical principles and practices. The result is a spiritually-based long-term strategic framework. This framework is called Blessed Strategy. Blessed Strategy is a spiritually-based strategic framework embedded in biblical principles that guides you in developing and executing business actions and measuring the result of those actions. The reason that I mention this is because you need to know what to expect. The Blessed Strategy framework is open to anyone that is interested in spiritually-based leadership principles, and is considering starting and building a spiritually-based business. Yet, it is targeted explicitly toward the entrepreneur or business owner who is seeking to re-develop and scale their business based on spiritual values and principles. My personal connection to these principles is from a biblical perspective, yet feel free to connect and relate the content to a spiritual perspective that is comfortable and appropriate for you and is based on your spiritual model and is appropriate for your business. My goal is to facilitate access to the power of spiritual and biblical principles for your business; it is not to advocate a single perspective of spirituality. I hope you are excited about undertaking and exploring the benefit of having a Blessed Strategy framework. I am excited for you.

With all of this, let's get started.

The Problem

I realize that books aimed toward business owners are not uncommon. In fact, much of the information provided in these books is redundant and can even be found for little or no cost. Yet, it is rare that these books focus on the strategic long-term success of a business based on spiritual and biblical principles in an explicit sense. Further, business plans and non-profit organizations offering business advice, as valuable as they are, generally focus on the short-term tactical elements of business development with an emphasis on obtaining start-up funding and building a network of professionals. That is important information; it's so important that I encourage you to review the literature and attend the events they offer. However, as valuable as the information provided, the core problem remains unresolved. That core problem is this: *entrepreneurs and current business owners are not generally positioning their business in a formalized, strategic way that furthers their business for long-term success based on enduring spiritual and biblical principles.*

In consulting, serving, and speaking with small business owners across the nation, and from teaching in various colleges over the years, I found that a focused strategic, long-term growth roadmap that equips business owners and leaders with the skills, knowledge, and tools, based on spiritual principles, was missing from most courses and resources. Sure, there were fragments of information available in higher learning institutions, seminars, and college programs; however, obtaining focused information, within the mainstream literature, that was affordable and delivered to meet the strategic needs of business owners was missing. Further, there may be an assumption that the effort needed to put together an individual roadmap that incorporated spiritually-based principles and focused strategy planning takes time away from what the business owner needs to focus on, which is scaling their business, ensuring that it meets some spiritual aim above and beyond profit.

Related to that problem, business owners generally lack comprehensive knowledge on how to develop and implement strategic plans and control mechanisms that monitor the health of the business, alerting them to possible forces and pressures that pose as emergent threats. When probing deeper, I found something more important and critical: that most business owners do not possess the necessary expertise or skillset needed to achieve long-term success – and that is a big problem.

Lack of will or an inability to learn is not the problem. In fact, evidence of learning by hardworking and extremely intelligent entrepreneurs is common; indeed, it's a case where the entrepreneur and the organization, in a sense, defines the framework, or at least sets the context for the problem. We, as entrepreneurs, demonstrate tenacity and resilience that should be applauded. Yet, there comes a time when the business must scale and assume a life independent from the owner, in order to reach its full potential. I am confident that most business owners would love to pass down their business to their sons or daughters, or position the business for sale, or even take the business public. And, if this logic applies to you, then you are reading the right book.

The Value

So the question comes down to, "How is Blessed Strategy different?" The answer is quite simple: Blessed Strategy compels you to take action… action that is based upon your spiritual identity that I think will prove to be the tipping point for your business. Here are four specific areas emphasized in the Blessed Strategy framework that you will be able to immediately apply to your business.

Spiritually-Based and Biblical Principles: It is my firm belief that the literature, workshops, and mainstream literature on strategy is good and necessary, but not sufficient. Because we are now in an interconnected, global business environment that has operated on industrial-based designs for over a century, multiple approaches to strategy planning and execution were developed. Some of these approaches have been successful. In the U.S. and other countries that are influenced by U.S. and Western European business development, the approach was to build upon industrial-based models made famous by Frederick Taylor, Elton Mayo, and Michael Porter. Yet too much has changed to remain dogmatically tied to these models. There are other models that have advanced the views of these business researchers, yet for entrepreneurs that seek (and don't mind, indeed look for) a spiritually-based strategic framework, there remains a void. Blessed Strategy fills that void.

Visioning and Strategic Planning: One often hears the concept of visioning and strategic planning – in fact, many erroneously equate every action as being strategic in nature. There is certainly no shortage of business owners that I meet that have some experience in visioning and strategic planning; yet, what I find is that most small business owners lack a robust or complete visioning and strategic planning process within their businesses. This book will not just merely cover these concepts, you will work on these concepts in real-time, which enables you to gain needed insight that you can apply as you go.

Monitoring and Controls: In visiting and speaking with numerous business owners and small business employees, I find that 1 out of 3 businesses are in a position to grow in a significant way. What I mean here is that the infrastructure is in place to leverage economies of scale and extend the business beyond its current scope of operations. That's the good news. The bad news is that these business owners are not aware of this window of opportunity or lack the expertise on how to leverage their business structure. There is also a lack of how to rigorously develop and execute growth strategies and assess potential risk. Also missing is insight into how to implement business monitors and controls, while also "looping" learning back into the business. Within this book, you will be armed with information in this area, building and implementing actual monitors and controls relevant to your business.

Integrating Staff Functions and Technology: One of the most glaring omissions from many small businesses is the absence of, and often unwillingness to, integrate staff functions and technology into the business infrastructure. When I inquire into this, I find that much of the hesitancy points toward the belief that technology and specialized staff support plans and strategies equate to high cost. Important here is to dispel myth and address the issue. First is the myth that technology and staff support equates to excessive cost with little to no returns. The truth is that technology investments, in many cases, can be efficiently implemented and do provide a tangible return with considerable positive impact. Blessed Strategy shows you how to consider technology investments alongside other capital investments and determine an investment return. In addition, Blessed Strategy shows you why it is important for you to know your technology and workforce requirements, and how incorporating these elements in the startup or early stages of your business lifecycle is critical to delivering on what your customers and clients expect from you and your business. In sum, you will learn how to incorporate staff functions and relevant technology into your business in its early stages.

Linkage of Strategy to Business Operations: Without the capability to link strategy to business operations, it isn't a matter of when your business will cease to grow, it's a matter of when. Furthermore, and just as unfortunate, operations without strategy is just a job, and you did not enter the ranks of entrepreneur and business owner, one can assume, just to have a job. Being an entrepreneur means having an ability to step outside the business and truly enjoy and benefit from the sweat, labor, and love you invested. I have spoken with business owners that love being inside the business, and that's fine. However, it does not negate the fact (a) your business needs to have formalized processes that incorporate long-term planning into focused action plans that can be tracked; and, (b) you owe it to yourself and your employees to build a stable business that positively impacts customers, employees, and the community. In order to accomplish this, you will have to be able to link strategic planning into actionable plans. These plans and actions have to extend beyond the few pages dedicated to it in your initial business plan; this linkage must be embedded into the fabric and DNA of your business… from the start.

The Benefit

There are additional benefits to Blessed Strategy, which include:

- Recognizing and understanding the spiritual connection between you and your business
- Learning how to incorporate social responsibility during the startup and early growth phases of your business
- Learning to leverage business learning and knowledge
- Understanding the importance of making capital investments and reaping economic profits
- The role of continuous improvement

. . . and so much more!

Important Note

As mentioned earlier, I strongly believe that businesses should exist to truly serve, which is why Blessed Strategy was developed. Blessed Strategy is built upon a premise that the true value of a business is its impact on customers, employees, and the community. Blessed Strategy is written for entrepreneurs and business owners that feel it is important for their businesses to operate from a spiritually-based framework that acknowledges God, community, and family.

Let's get down to scope.

Scope

Blessed Strategy covers a lot of ground, yet does have bounds. At its core, Blessed Strategy is focused on spiritually-based strategy planning and implementation for entrepreneurs and small business owners. The book makes the following assumptions:

- **An existing business entity**: Though Blessed Strategy can prove very useful to the entrepreneur at the idea stage (in fact, there is a section at the end in which we will discuss this concept). It assumes that your business exists and that it is in the early stages of operation, or at the very least, you have experience in starting and developing a business.
- **A desire to achieve spiritually-based breakthroughs**: Blessed Strategy assumes that you, as the owner(s) or a key leader, are looking to achieve breakthrough by focusing on the development of a spiritually-based strategy and implementation of that strategy. Blessed Strategy covers positioning your company for long-term strategic success. Further, Blessed Strategy assumes that you believe in spiritually-based principles and values, and also believe (or are open to believing) that these spiritual dimensions are critical to long-term business success.
- **Business serves a purpose**: You hear a lot about the purpose-driven organization and business with a purpose. Blessed Strategy not only supports that notion, it expounds upon it in a very detailed and specific manner, framed by spiritually-based principles and values.
- **Recognition of the value of action**: There are a lot of dreamers that take no action. Blessed Strategy assumes that you are a doer, who is focused on building a business that will last. Though you will likely be motivated and inspired in reading this book, you are

also going to be very active. Blessed Strategy focuses you on taking action. The results of your efforts will be a long-term strategy roadmap that consist of short-term action plans that guides your business to long-term success.

Limitations

Just as important as telling you what this series is, it's also important to tell you what it's not. Blessed Strategy is not a guide to establishing start-up concerns such as dream-teaming, networking, or generating ideas, although you may be inspired in those areas. There are no long discussions on how to select your lawyer, accountant, or other team of advisers. There are important references to these areas, yet, there are no specific guidance in these matters. Next, there is not an extended discussion on business structuring. The assumption Blessed Strategy holds is that your business is already in operation, or at least close to opening "the doors," thus the formation element is not addressed. There **is** insight into how to best leverage, position, or re-position your business; yet, business formation requires important **detailed** consideration, and this discussion is best done in consultation with your lawyer and accountant. Similarly, there is no extended discussion on tax-related issues, or issues related to debt-equity structuring. There are some discussions on capital funding, venture capital, and debt-equity structuring as it relates to business growth; however, the in-depth initial discussions on those issues are best left to your professional financial and legal teams.

Disclaimer

This book is not designed to provide legal or accounting advice. Please ensure that you consult with your lawyer and accountant for those areas in which their expertise is required or recommended.

CHAPTER 1

Understanding and Connecting with Your Personal and Business Core

*Agree with God, and be at peace; thereby good
will come to you* - Job 22:21 (KJV)

Your business exists for a purpose.

Whatever that purpose happens to be, you must know and remain connected to that purpose from the time you start your business to the moment you sell or pass that business on to others – and oftentimes, even longer – you never know when you may be called back – Howard Schultz, anyone?! In the popular press, this is often referred to as understanding your core – your reason for being, the very reason for your business's existence. Now many of you may say (and for some you actually do): *my core is to develop my product and make money.* Yet, what I am talking about goes much deeper than that, and going deeper makes a difference and does matter. So what does understanding your core mean in context of what is presented for our purposes? It means understanding why you and your business exists beyond profit; it involves understanding the impact of your business to society, community, and employees, and the benefit of your goods and services, and the connection between you, your business, and your stakeholders.

Why does this matter?

It matters because when you start a business, you are starting an entity that is a part of you, yet extends beyond you. Your business will reside within a community in which competing stakeholder claims will be made and you must decide *who* and *what* warrants your attention at any given moment. Your business will have opportunities to extend in related and unrelated areas, and you must understand who you are and what your business represents. There will be times when your business will be stretched and competitors emerge, investors become impatient, and cash flow slows. You will need to know, in your spirit and soul, just what the business means to you and to its stakeholders.

It's no longer a secret, businesses that understand their purpose, their reason for being, beyond and above profit are looked upon favorably because they act ethically and execute strategies deliberately and with purpose. Peter Senge, in his great book, *The Fifth Discipline* writes (and continues to talk) about the importance of understanding your core and the spiritual connection between you and your business as does his protégé Otto Scharmer in *Theory U*. Longstanding entrepreneurs and business leaders, such as Howard Schultz of Starbucks and Arne Sorenson of Marriott International are testaments of the spiritual connection within successful businesses and recognizing your core purpose.

In consulting and speaking with countless entrepreneurs and businesses owners, I conclude that understanding your personal core and your spiritual connection does provide an intrinsic advantage that comes forth within decisions made, processes executed, and systems employed, that lead to a competitive advantage. You will need to believe and understand this to gain the most benefit from the Blessed Strategy framework.

Activity 1 – Personal Spiritual Statement

Take a moment to write your spiritual statement. Keep this statement short (no more than 3 sentences). For those of you thinking ahead, this is not your mission statement; however, it does follow a similar format. It should be short; you should be able to remember this statement; it should be meaningful to you. It should be internalized into the very fabric of your being.

_____

_____

_____

_____

_____

_____

Activity 2 – Personal Spiritual Statement and Business Connection

Take a moment to write how your personal spiritual statement you've written above is connected to your business. Be specific and clear. This statement may be longer than your personal spiritual statement, but it doesn't need to be – that is up to you. The important thing is to make it concrete and clear. To make it where you can come back to it in a year or ten years and still understand the connection.

_____

_____

_____

_____

_____

Take a moment to reflect. Reflect on all great leaders and what made them great from a spiritual perspective. Jesus, for example, was a great leader.

His spirit remained after He was crucified, and the Disciples continued to work with Jesus' spirit embedded into the fabric of who they were as they continued following his teachings. We can see recent examples of the power of a leader's spirit in companies such as Apple. Much is written about the great technical insight and business understanding of Steve Jobs, yet few recognize just how much time he spent, especially in the last few years of his life, building a spirit within Apple. A spirit that was a part of him yet would extend beyond him, after he died. A spirit of innovation and a spirit of recognizing customer needs, while leveraging human capability. It's that spirit that enabled Apple to continue successfully competing within an industry that is highly competitive.

When you build a spirit within your company, understand that this spirit extends beyond you. When you read the bible, the Spirit of God enables you to learn multiple things from a single passage at different times when you need it. When you buy an Apple product, you recognize the spirit of innovation integrated with simplicity. When you visit the White House, you feel the democratic spirit of our nation's founding fathers that still guides country today. If you take a moment to reflect, you recognize that great leaders and entrepreneurs think about the meaning, purpose, and feeling their legacy and businesses will mean to multiple groups – multiple stakeholders. You will also likely recognize that this spirit attracts people that will enable the spirit created to live on. Think about that for a moment. Close your eyes and think about your company living for a decade, twenty years, or even, a century beyond you – yet it still is a part of you, your vision come to life.

Activity 3 –Business-to-Stakeholder Spiritual Connection

Now take a moment to write how your business is spiritually connected (or how you envision it to be connected) to its stakeholders. Think about how your business is spiritually connected to its customers, to the community, and to society. Again, be specific and clear. Close your eyes and think of the moral and societal value that your company has or will provide. Important in this activity is to picture your company through the eyes of your customer, supplier, distributor, and even your competition. What does this spirit look like in action? What does it feel like? Go for it.

_____

_____

_____

_____

_____

_____

Let's take a moment to extend our metaphysical exploration into a more concrete discussion. Remember when you first had that idea for your business. If you are like many entrepreneurs, you talked about it day-in and day-out. You could imagine all the details of the product and service that would be offered, and you had a picture in your mind of what the business would look like. You had some concept of a customer and thoughts of how your business would deliver on customers' expectations, and you may have even considered how you would exceed those expectations. For those truly visionary entrepreneurs, you may have even considered how you would redefine markets and industries and impact lifestyles. It was a great feeling, was it not?! Thank about it for a second. You were excited, passionate, and focused. Hopefully, you still are. Okay – reel it in.

Let's revisit that moment for a second. However (as hard as it may be), I need you to be critical for a second. I need you to imagine yourself in a room full of mini-you(s), throw in a couple of investors, a customer group, and some community stakeholders. They are all sitting around you, telling you to explain your business and its product. They ask you to tell them how your business is connected to you and to your customers. Imagine that you are hearing such statements such as, "I understand Ms. Johnson, but again, what does this mean to me?" Or, "Just who will benefit from your product or service?" Now with that image in your mind, I want you to think of your company, once again for many of you, considering these factors:

- Business Core Purpose
- My Business Spiritual Purpose
- My Business Benefits
- My Business Serves
- Me-and-My Business Connection
- My Business-to-Stakeholder Connection

Activity 4 – Business Core Statement

_____

_____

_____

_____

_____

_____

You have accomplished a lot in our first section – and just think, you are just beginning. You are just scratching the surface of what will be a series of readings, reflections, and activities that will get you energized again and refocused on your business. Also, you will be armed with information that you can immediately act on. In fact, I encourage you to reflect on each exercise and adjust as you go along and revisit throughout our time together.

Summary

The primary objective of this chapter was for you to consider *for what purpose does my business exist, above and beyond profit*? Not necessarily a new question yet, for our purposes, the basis of this question was to go beyond a social responsibility or ethics perspective and consider how your business connects with your spiritual self. Upon exploring your business in connection with your spiritual self, you had an opportunity to develop spiritually-based personal and business statements. The aim of the statements was to make a focused effort to connect (or reconnect) your business to who you are as individual and spiritual being, laying a spiritual foundation. Building upon that spiritual foundation, you had a chance to reflect on your business and its purpose inclusive of, yet beyond profit. This reflection included consideration of you and your business' stakeholders to include employees, customers, and communities. This reflection and the accompanying exercises helped to position you for the spiritually-based strategic journey ahead, as you work to develop a Blessed Strategy that connects you and your business to an enduring spiritual purpose and legacy.

CHAPTER 2

What is Your Business About and Where is it Going?!

Whether you turn to the rigor or to the left, your ears will hear a voice behind you saying, "That is the way; walk in it" – Isaiah 30:21 (KJV)

When one speaks of mission and vision, the heads nod in agreement, and the eyes light-up in understanding. Business owners and managers often tell us, "Yeah, we got it; vision is the future ideal state, and mission is who we are and what we are about; we got it; we got it." Yet, when I probe deeper, what I find is that these owners and managers and the businesses that they lead often do not have it. Or better yet, some know it, but don't have it nor feel any pressing need to get it. A few business owners and managers may think they are deeply familiar with visioning, only to find out that their current mission or vision is not known or bought into by employees and other key stakeholders. Others just don't see a need for it, and if you fall under this category, I hope that by the end of this section, I can convince you otherwise.

Here is the deal: being familiar with the concept in words is not enough. To know *who you are* and *what you are about* requires that you also know that your mission and vision are bigger than you. Remember early where you started to get to this point: you started by taking a very personalized view of who you were and how this extended to your business. Once that connection was made, you found that your business core and purpose must also connect with other key internal and external factors. To make this connection, you had to walk-back to the beginning. You had to ask yourself, *just what is my business about and where is it heading?*

Before advancing too far ahead, let's explore how this process is customarily handled within businesses, large and small. Business owners, senior executives and managers, and key employees come together and frame a series of statements often referred to as organizational statements. Hours (and sometimes days and weeks) are spent going back to the values and to the "core," and bringing key elements into these statements to maintain relevance in the current context of the business operations. A couple of statements (mission and vision) and perhaps, a value statement is developed and shared across the company. In complex organizations, this process may be supplemented by divisional and departmental efforts. The statements are published in various work areas, hallways, and organizational boards throughout the company and then... forgotten about. That's right, forgotten about. I can walk through some of your companies right now, and I would find that many employees do not know the statements, and if I am fortunate to get past that point on the rare occasions that employees may able to remember the contents of the statements, there is rarely an ability to articulate a concrete connection between their efforts and the mission and vision of the company.

And that's your problem.

Yet, you can fix this by doing a little reverse engineering. You ended the last section by making a connection to what your company means to your stakeholders from a spiritual perspective. You were connecting the core of who you are to your business and how your business connects with its stakeholders. Now you need to walk that back, and connect who you are to help determine your ideal future state.

Why are am I recommending this approach? As a small-to-medium size business owner and entrepreneur, you are unique. Not yet in the Fortune 500 or a large privately-held company, your mission and vision needs to be personalized, yet also expansive, inclusive, and shared. In other words, the ownership of these statements at the beginning stages is yours. In addition, the responsibility for buy-in, understanding, and connection is also yours. As your business grows, you will come to find that there are multiple approaches to developing your business statements. You will also discover that there are various approaches to get to the same goal; that there is more than one way to get to the destination. However, in this approach, you will complete specific tasks, in what may be, for some, counter-intuitive objectives. The goal is to ensure that you are authentically connected to your organizational statements, while also ensuring that the statements extend beyond you.

Review your Chapter One activities. Reflect on how your business connects with its stakeholders. Think about the benefits that your business provides to society, the community, to customers, and employees. Think about the experience you will deliver to your customers and how you will consistently provide that experience and deliver on (and even exceed) customer expectations. Think about the spiritual bond that connects stakeholders to your business and your business to you. Review your business core statement. Keep walking back, close your eyes, and ask yourself, *what is my business about?*

Activity 1 – Personal Mission Statement

Take a moment to write your personal mission statement. What is your purpose and mission in life? You laid the groundwork in Chapter 1, and you also have the benefit of reflection. Allow me to share my personal mission statement to move us along. My personal mission statement is: *To provide, acquire, and share knowledge that will benefit people and improve businesses and communities.* It's that simple and that clean. It's not the mission statement for my business, yet it serves as input for my business mission statement. Now, it's your turn. What is your personal mission statement – remember to account for the factors mentioned above.

_____

_____

_____

_____

_____

_____

Now take a moment to reflect on your personal mission statement, while considering the holistic perspective introduced in Chapter 1 and in the beginning of this section, and draft your business mission statement (Note: If there are multiple business owners, each business owner should write a personal mission statement and draft an individual business mission statement). Allow me to provide you another example. EntOrgCorp's mission statement is: *Delivering inspiration and providing insight through focused strategy development and innovative leading-edge technology solutions.* Note the alignment between my personal mission statement and that of my company, EntOrgCorp. Now take a moment to reflect and develop a draft of your business statement. Have at it.

Activity 2 – Business Mission Statement

_____

_____

_____

_____

_____

_____

Now if your business has more than one owner, you will collaborate with your partner and develop a single mission statement draft that considers your individual statements as input.

As your business lifecycle advances, this process will become even more intensive and inclusive for as your business grows so does the need for *buy-in* from multiple stakeholders, especially your employees. Your statements will need to align with the hopes, aspirations, and dreams of your employees as well as your own. For now, you will continue to refine this statement during this chapter and advance to the next major objective.

****

Much has been written about the role, place, and impact of vision in history. You can find multiple instances ranging from the Bible to politics to the arts to science and entertainment. One of my favorite verses from the Bible reads, "And a vision appeared to Paul in the night: There stood a man of Macedonia, and prayed him, saying, 'Come over into Macedonia and help us (Acts 16:9 KJV).'" The reason that verse is so important is because it speaks to an ideal future state.

One of the most important examples of vision in business is found in Henry Ford. The Henry Ford (2010), a nonprofit organization dedicated to information of value to the education and business community, writes, "Ford demonstrated one of the most important characteristics – the ability to articulate a vision and convince other people to sign on and help him achieve that vision.[2]" Ford is recognized for not only recognizing the value of vision, but also is known for reshaping and actively revisiting vision. After successfully bringing the Model N to market, he articulated a vision to develop a motorcar that was affordable to the general public.

Consider this statement made by Ford:

> *...will build a motor car for the great multitude.*
> *It will be large enough for the family but*

small enough for the individual to run and care for. It will be constructed of the best materials, by the best men to be hired, after the simplest designs that modern engineering can devise. But it will be so low in price that no

---

[2] The Henry Ford (2010). *Visionaries on Innovation*. https://www.thehenryford.org

man making a good salary will be unable to own one—and enjoy with
his family the blessings of hours of pleasure in God's great open spaces[3].

Note how powerful and clear Ford's vision was in reflecting on the above statement. You can picture his vision in vivid detail. His vision touches on several concepts covered thus far in *Blessed Strategy*. It makes a connection to society, notably the family unit. It brings forward the role of human capital in making the vision possible, and most importantly, it makes a spiritual connection. Just as your business mission is aligned with your business core, your spiritual purpose, and your personal mission, so is the case with your vision. Yet, your vision is also unique. It is a powerful and a foundational element of your business planning. Many of you already have such statements within your business plan… and that's good. However, you need to revisit these. Take a moment to consider your business vision alongside your personal spiritual statement, business purpose (above and beyond profit), and your business-to-stakeholder connections.

Before moving on in developing or refining your business vision, some additional points about vision are important to consider. First, there are many personal approaches to vision. Some companies combine vision and mission statements; some business owners see little need in such statements; and some businesses think that visions should be very specific, while other business owners go for inspirational vision statements. My intent is not to dispute any of these philosophical approaches, instead, my emphasis on vision is rooted in the role of vision throughout history. What I've seen in high-performing organizations (business, public sector, and non-profit) is the common ideal state that can communicate concrete meaning and purpose across key stakeholder groups.

Next, there are debates on just what is the role of organizational vision. Just as the approach to developing a mission statement can range from a single person to an executive group to multiple stakeholders, so too can the vision statement. Where you, as the start-up entrepreneur or small business owner, you need to focus on developing an *outward-in approach*. With the *outward-in approach*, you will again consider the business-to-stakeholder

---

[3] The Henry Ford (2010). *Visionaries on Innovation.* https://www.thehenryford.org

dynamic, and how this relates to you as the business owner. The reason is because at this stage of your business cycle, your vision should be personalized, yet also inclusive and shared. It's important for you – for all of us – to understand just how powerful vision can be for ourselves, our employees, our investors, and our communities. Powerful vision statements invoke emotion, enhance commitment, and create a common drive toward a specific purpose. Strong vision statements are lasting, yet are not dogmatic or inflexible. Inspiring visions connect employees and owners, customers and investors. The best visions align behaviors that make the attainment of the ideal possible.

Having said this, let's get started on developing or revisiting your business vision statement based, on your collective insights and reflections thus far.

Activity 3 – Business Vision Statement

_____

_____

_____

_____

_____

_____

Please note that you will have opportunities to revisit your vision at a later time – and for that matter, this can be done at any time throughout your business lifecycle. In closing out this activity for now, remember to not underestimate the power of vision. Vision signifies an ideal, vision represents unified purpose, and vision compels you and your team to act. An effective vision statement propels you and your business toward execution of actions consistent and supportive of achieving the vision. Effective visions are both personal and shared. Visions are ideally spiritual and engaging. Senge (2006) states that "[v]isions are exhilarating. They create the spark, the excitement that lifts an organization[4]." I could not agree more, and it is my hope that you were reinvigorated going through this process.

****

Now with the mission and vision statements revisited based on a spiritual-based paradigm and a shared perspective, you are now ready to consider (or reconsider) the values that drive you and your business. Values are another one of the core strategic business concepts that you need to embrace. Often dismissed as mumbo-jumbo, gibberish, or fuzzy talk, the development and role-modeling of your company's values is arguably one of the most important undertakings pursued in business – especially from a long-term perspective. Values are the spirit in which actions and tasks are carried out. Values guide employee-to-employee, manager-to-employee, and employee-to-customer interactions. Your business values are more than just bumper stickers. Your company's values serve as the foundation of interactions and conduct; they signify what you stand for and the spirit in which exchanges should take place. Values serve as the bounds of behaviors. Your business values are the mechanism that governs conduct and serves as an indicator of your business culture. It's not soft or fuzzy. Values matter. If my statements are not powerful enough for you, take a moment to review what former IBM Chief Executive Officer, Sam Palmisano, said about values:

> [Y]ou've got to create a management system that empowers people and provides a basis of decision-making consistent with who [you are]. Values inject balance in the management system – balance between the short-term transaction and long-term relationship, balance between the interests of shareholders, employees, and clients. Values help you make

---

[4] Senge (2006). The Fifth Discipline: The Art and Practice of the Learning Organization. p. 194.

those decisions in a way that is consistent with who you are as a company[5].

Values are not only reserved for large, complex companies. In fact, the most important starting point for values is in the beginning. Great entrepreneurs that are serious in building a company with a lasting legacy and soul obsess over values. These entrepreneurs know that values are the endearing elements that will remain long after your retire; they help articulate the legacy you are building. These are the core elements of your company that future owners will refer to during times of challenge and change. Your business values are felt by your customers and extend to the community and society. Your business values are signals that welcome those that share your values and serve as a caution to individuals and groups whose values may not align with yours.

You may not realize it; however, since you started reading this book, you have set the foundation for your values. Don't believe me?! Take a moment to review your work thus far. You have worked hard on not only developing and revisiting your business, you have also worked hard in re-discovering who you are – exploring your core, examining your connection to your business and your business's connection to its community. You pushed forward and walked backward to ensure alignment, and with all this work done, you now have a starting point to begin developing your business values as an entrepreneur.

Now if you could integrate this foundational schema into a core set of values, what would those values be? What are the descriptors that govern you and your employees' interactions? What should the customer see and feel when conducting business with your company? Take a moment to write six to eight descriptors that represent your values. Examples of values that still connect with me personally and professionally are the Navy's values of *Honor, Courage,* and *Commitment.* These organizational values are simple, yet powerful, longstanding and galvanizing. Let's get started.

---

[5] "How IBM's Sam Palmisano Redefined the Global Corporation, 2012 January 18, *Harvard Business Review*

Activity 4 – Business Value Descriptors

_____ _____ _____ _____

_____ _____ _____ _____

****

Take a moment to reflect on the great companies you have conducted business with as a customer, business partner, or client. What elements of the company made these companies great in your perspective? Was it their customer service? Was it the way a problem was addressed and resolved? What about the way the company served its communities and acted with a sense of responsibility and accountability? If these things mattered to you, then you can assume that your customers are looking for similar experiences – and they are. Your customers and clients are endeared to more than just a product or service; they are endeared to what you and your company stand for, especially in the case of customers that have a significant lifetime value. They see your values in action. They see the standards of behavior and the efforts your business puts forth, checking for consistency and execution with purpose. Your values serve to guide the actions that represent your personal and business purpose and role, above and beyond profit. Values represent the connection that endears customers, investors, and community to your company; the manner in which these specific actions are pursued – your company's values in motion – are your company's ethics. Social responsibility is the specific, concrete efforts that provide evidence of your company's view of its obligations above and beyond (yet can be inclusive of) profit. Both of which will be discussed next.

Role of Ethics

Related to values is your business's commitment to ethics. In practice, ethics can be needlessly complicated in many ways. There are approaches to ethics that cloud the theory and work to complicate what should be a straightforward concept. Fortunately, you have the framework for your ethical framework already established. Necessary is some discussion, before getting into the work of framing your business ethical model.

The first question centers on answering one question, and that question is this: *What are ethics?* Ethics are the internal rule-set that governs one's behavior. So being ethical means to do the right thing, the right way, all the time. Business ethics is doing the right thing, the right way, all the time in business. Your personal ethical framework should align with your business ethical framework, just as your business core aligned with your purpose statements. It amazes me when entrepreneurs and business professionals (some very senior) mixed compliance with ethics. It is this shortcoming that these owners, managers, and professionals use to cloud conduct. Some say there is a thin line between compliance and ethics, and that perspective is absolutely absurd. Compliance is meeting the requirements and is outcome-focused. Ethics are focused on the process and the outcome within the context of where an act is being considered and performed.

Personal ethics are YOUR values in motion. With that in mind, your business ethics, as an extension of your personal ethics, are your business values in execution. It's really that simple… in words. This is one reason why having a business that stems from a spiritual purpose and is connected morally to key stakeholders is important. Next, I want you to think about this for a moment: imagine that you are called away from your business, for whatever reason. Perhaps, your company wants you to sit on a committee. Perhaps, you need to take care of a parent full-time. Perhaps, you just want to get away. In any case, you will be gone for quite some time. Can you honestly say that your business from an ethical perspective would reflect you? Do your employees know the value of ethics in your business and are your personal ethics aligned with your business ethics? Be honest.

I look for ethics in the majority of my business transactions and your customers do, too. I want to be assured that you are properly preparing and disposing of waste when no one is looking. I want to know that you are not merely *complying* with financial laws and *SEC* regulations when releasing financial statements; I want you to think of this as *your* investment dollars at work. When we think about ethics from these principles based on the golden rule of *do unto others,* then it doesn't become as complicated as some may suggest. Here is a sobering finding: just as we all sin, at some point in time, one's conduct is unethical. Yes – that means you (and me). Now, I am not here to judge. Maybe you do take pens from work. Maybe you did have someone complete your college paper without input from you. Maybe you did misrepresent your income on your tax return. The point is that unethical actions and behavior were likely executed by you (and me) at some point in time. Part of our responsibilities as entrepreneurs is to minimize unethical conduct and to prevent unethical behaviors that contribute to a dysfunctional business. Your responsibility is to hold your employees both accountable and responsible for ethical behavior. It is your responsibility to role-model ethical conduct in all communication, actions, and behaviors. Is it a tall order at times? Yes – we are human, and as humans, we have interests, and these interests will oftentimes be at odds with what's right. But you have a decision to make, and when you work to act ethically consistently every day, it becomes ingrained in you. When your employees see it, they witness your commitment to ethics. When your customers see it, they feel good about doing business with you.

Now let's proceed to develop or refine your ethics statement. You have quite a bit of technology (in the form of statements) in front of you now, so we will need to employ that technology to develop an inclusive, ethical statement that aligns with who we are, your business core purpose, and considers your business stakeholders. Place, your mission statement, spiritual purpose statement, business core statement, and social responsibility statement at the center, and place the remaining statements on the outer-edges of these statements. Read and reflect on these statements. Ready?! Let's go. Develop or refine your business ethics statement.

Activity 6 – Business Ethics Statement

_____

_____

_____

_____

_____

_____

Why is this important? One reason is because different individuals and groups have different expectations, and your customers can play a different role, depending on location and circumstances. I will never forget sitting on a training session for the U.S. Post Office, and the facilitator made a remark that she is an employee when at work and is a customer when she arrives home. This seemingly simple statement has profound implications. One moment, she is training peers and new hires, and when she arrives home, she is looking for a timely and reliable delivery of mail. In one role, she represents the values and is executing a form of responsibility, and in the other, she observes the values and the spirit of service, and integration of the two.

Now, let's think about the role your business currently has in the community. If you own a restaurant, your customers want a meal and experience that is consistent with your brand. Your suppliers are looking for a reliable customer that will buy seasoning, cleaning supplies, food items, menu laminators, beverage items, and so forth. The school may look to you as both a reliable employer and a training ground for emerging leaders. And the list goes on and on. These expectations and claims are valid and fair, so it's important to think about this not when you scale, but when you open the doors. These expectations matter. Advance economic theories often refer to multiple expectations put on a business as competing claims. In plain language, what this simply means is that your business, as we've covered extensively, has expectations from various stakeholder groups. The expectations are dynamic and fluid, and you need to know when and how you will address these expectations. This is one of the reasons why I wanted you to put a considerable amount of thought and time in the beginning at identifying your business core. In any case, it's important that you remember: these expectations are healthy, valid, and fair. Don't ignore them.

Now, *Blessed Strategy*, is an entrepreneur's spiritual strategic planning guide, and though the principles related to MBAs apply, this is not an MBA program. So let's get to some specific, concrete entrepreneur translations of social responsibility and a helpful schematic that you can apply. There are two ways to divide social responsibility. There is what is called *Good Manners Expectations* on one side, and on the other side, *Specialized Expectations* (see below).

Good Manners Expectations	Specialized Expectations

Now, let's take an example of a local auto body shop. The owner of the shop operates a body shop that generates $500,000 in annual revenue. The body shop has a six-person staff consisting of the owner, four body shop technicians, and an administrative assistant. The shop is in its fourth year of being in business and has a steady workflow consisting of insurance claimants, wholesales and renovators, used car lots, and individual customers. The owner is a well-known entrepreneur known for dedicating her time to various causes in the community.

There will be various claims put on the business. First, there is the customer claim on the company that good quality body work be provided, yet there are also additional expectations (claims) that customers seek. One expectation may be to hire local talent, skilled and experienced in auto body repair. To add a layer of consideration, the owner's shop is located in a highly diverse neighborhood; so not only do customers want talented and skilled employees that are local, they may want a workforce that reflects the local community. Next, you have community members that care deeply about the environment and are concerned with the company's responsible use and disposal of hazard waste, so another claim from the community (that can include a customer) is to responsibly dispose of hazardous material. Our Good Manners Expectations and Specialized Expectations now look like this:

Good Manners Expectations	Specialized Expectations
• **Hire from local community** • **Diverse workforce**	• **Dispose of hazardous materials** • **Recycle of useable materials**

As you can see, in this simplified example, there are multiple claims placed on the business. A business that is successful, yet is also limited in resources. This brings forward an important point: being socially responsible can be difficult but does not have to be rocket science. Perhaps, one of the most important considerations is to recognize both the economic and accounting impact of being socially responsible. Let's go a little deeper here. There are some efforts related to your social responsibility efforts that will require a cash outlay or expenditure (an accounting action). In our body shop example, the auto mechanic uses high-quality paint that exceeds insurance requirements. The reason for this is because the high-quality paint allows the owner to deliver on customer quality expectations, and in addition, the chemicals used are transparent and facilitate proper disposal. In addition, the owner has not one, but two hazardous waste stations that allow employees in both bays to properly dispose of waste without leaving the bay area. This keeps traffic organized and safe and provides a safe work environment (an additional expectation of the employee).

Now to implement these processes is beyond compliance. Despite these costs, the owner feels that pursing these efforts is the right thing to do and allows her to meet the expectations that are both implied and explicit. The question is will she see a return? Maybe and ideally, she would. The challenge becomes just when is there a return generated by her company. In many cases, you will not know; however, one can reasonably assume that there is a long-term return on the effort, at some point, because our auto shop owner is addressing the expectations placed upon the firm above-and-beyond profit. Important for us to know is that there are two returns to consider:

Economic Return: There is an opportunity cost associated with pursuing efforts that go beyond compliance, and when these opportunities are pursued, a dollar obligated is one less dollar for marketing or toward additional incentive pay. Perhaps the dollar could have gone toward the bottom-line and reported as profits. However, by placing the dollar into an effort that is consistent with the owner's social responsibility objectives, the owner may realize an economic return above and beyond any short-term return from an alternative choice. A return that is realized in the long-run, which bring us to accounting returns.

Accounting Return: Accounting returns are generally associated with visible returns that can be tied to some financial metric and realized by your business in the short-term. You lease a new building, you can increase capacity therefore fulfilling more orders. The return from these efforts can be tied to measures that include internal rates-of-return, return-on-equity, or return-on-assets, to name a few of the metrics. In the above example, the owner understood the need to invest in long-term growth and considered both the short- and long-range aims of the business, the purchase of the building and the investment in equipment was determined based on pro forma(s), intense marketing research, and actual traffic in the shop as the years progressed. In short, our owner knew (with a reasonable degree of certainty) the income that the investment into her business would generate; yet, she also understood the need to invest in the long-term as well. She was comfortable with being able to tie in her return to concrete measures, yet was not dogmatic in tying down every single activity to a return when it came to doing what was right. She felt that would take care of itself, so long as the pursuit was strategic, consistent, pragmatic, and authentic.

When it comes to social responsibility, you don't quite know when the accounting return will come or quite honestly, if an accounting return is ever really generated. Yet (and this is important), the evidence over time shows that social responsibility does have a relationship with increased customer loyalty and positive brand awareness, resulting in long-term, sustainable earnings. The explicit evidence of effort may be found in positive local press and increased word-of-mouth. Allow me to share an important point made by Pearce and Robinson (2013):

> *The goal of every firm is to maintain viability through long-run profitability. Until all costs and benefits are accounted for,*

> *however, profits may not be claimed. In the case of* **corporate social responsibility (CSR)**, *costs and benefits are both economic and social. While economic costs and benefits are easily quantifiable, social costs and benefits are not*[6].

In reflecting on this, you can see why our earlier exercises were so important. Permit me to bring forward an important consideration: first, you may not know where to pinpoint the exact return for pursuing social responsibility efforts; however, if you know your personal and business purpose along with your spiritual connection and business core, the efforts you do pursue will align with you as an entrepreneur and your business. In other words, the social responsibility efforts you do pursue will be congruent with the aims that go above-and-beyond profit. The willingness to put forth these efforts is a little stronger than someone walking up to you and saying, "Hey, you should really look at a sustainability strategy for your business." This matters because you are still an entrepreneur, and as an entrepreneur, you know that the effort matters. As a spiritually-based entrepreneur with an explicit social responsibility strategy, the actions you take will be consistent with *who* you are. It is then reasonable to assume the results will reach your bottom-line, and in any case, you can conduct a purpose-driven risk assessment. With this framework in place, let's begin with our next activity.

Suffice it to say that this was indeed a comprehensive case for you to consider the role and impact of values and social responsibilities. For good reason, these are the elements of business where owners understand the importance of the values in theory; however, pursue a reactive approach to addressing the outcome and any changes. Your values and approach to social responsibility has to be ingrained in your company's DNA. So your efforts and reflections here are not for naught – far from it. Now, take a moment to develop or refine your business Social Responsibility Statement. Refer back to all your statements while placing your personal statement, business mission statement, and spiritual statements at the center. Aim for a statement that is specific, yet does not exceed five sentences.

---

[6] Pearce and Robinson (2013) Strategic Management (13th ed). p. 54

Activity 5 – Social Responsibility Statement

_____

_____

_____

_____

_____

_____

Related to social responsibility is your business's commitment to ethics. Ethics can be complicated in many ways. There are approaches to ethics that cloud theory and work to complicate what should be a straightforward concept. Fortunately, you have the framework for your ethical framework already established. Necessary, is some discussion before beginning the work in framing your business ethical model.

The first question centers on answer one question: *What is ethics?* Ethics is simply doing the right thing, all the time. Business ethics is doing the right thing all the time in business. Your personal ethical framework should align with your business ethical framework just as your business core statements aligned with your purpose statements. It amazes me when entrepreneurs and business professionals (some very senior) mix compliance with ethics. It is this shortcoming that these owners, managers, and professionals use to cloud conduct. Some say there is a thin line between compliance and ethics, and that perspective is absolutely absurd. Compliance is meeting the requirements and is outcome-focused. Ethics focus on the process and the outcome within the context of where the action is taking place.

Ethics are YOUR values in motion. Ethics are your values executed. With that in mind, your business ethics, as an extension of your personal ethics, are your business values in execution. It's really that simple… in words. This is one reason why having a business that stems from a spiritual purpose is important. Next, I want you to think about this for a moment. Imagine that you are called away for whatever reason. Perhaps, the U.S. President wants you to sit on a committee. Perhaps, you need to take care of a parent full-time. Perhaps, you just want to get away. In any case, you will be gone for quite some time. Do you think that your business, from an ethical perspective, would reflect you during your absence? Do your employees know the value of ethics in your business and are your personal ethics aligned with your business ethics? Be honest.

I look for ethics in the majority of my business transactions, and your customers do, too. I want to know that my business supplies are safe from *borrowing*. I want to know your track record in providing food that is properly prepared and disposed of when no one is looking. I want to know that you are not merely *complying* with financial laws and *SEC* regulations when releasing financial statements; I want you to think of this as your investment dollars at work. When we think about ethics from these principles based on the golden rule of *do unto others,* then it doesn't become as complicated as some may think. Here is a sobering finding: just as we all sin, at some point in time, our conduct is unethical. Yes – that means you and me. Now, I am not here to judge. Maybe you do take pens from work. Maybe you did have someone complete your college paper without input from you. Maybe you did misrepresent your income on your tax return. The point is that a degree of unethical behavior was likely executed by all of us, at some point in time. Part of our responsibilities (indeed obligations) as entrepreneurs and business owners is to minimize unethical conduct and to prevent unethical behaviors that cause dysfunction. Your responsibility is to hold your employees both accountable and responsible for ethical behavior and role model the ethics you want upheld. It is your responsibility to role model ethical conduct in communication, actions, and behaviors. Is it a tall order at times? Yes – we are human, and as humans, we have interests, and these interests will oftentimes be at odds with what's right. But you have a decision to make, and when you work to act ethically consistently every day, it becomes ingrained in you. When your employees see it, they witness your commitment to ethics. When your customers see it, they feel good about doing business with you.

Now you are ready to develop or refine your ethic statements. You have quite a bit of technology (in the form of statements) in front of you now, so we need to employ that technology to develop an inclusive, ethical statement that aligns with who you are, your business core purposes, and considers your business stakeholders. Place, your mission statement, spiritual purpose statement, business core statement, and social responsibility statement at the center, and place the remaining statements on the outer-edges of your work area. Read and reflect on these statements. Ready?! Let's go. Develop or refine your business ethics statement:

Activity 6 – Business Ethics Statement

_____

_____

_____

_____

_____

You have covered a lot of ground; yet there is still more visioning work to get done.

Let me start by asking you a very simple question: have you ever dealt with a broker? Brokers are everywhere. There are business brokers and real estate brokers; there are a business-real estate brokers, and the list goes on and on. The thing about a broker is that they work in your interest, yet are also independent of you. They have some degree of loyalty, yet there is a degree of autonomy as well. Brokers are in a position to tell backend providers when their products or services are in demand, the perception of their policies, and the perception of the company from a client perspective. Got that image? Good. Now, we need to extend that image. The first order of business is to imagine these brokers as committee members that work in your interest. Next, get rid of the word brokers since it contains the word *broke* - we are a prosperous group of leaders and thinkers.

These committees, of course, do in fact exist and are call boards. You will need a board not in five, ten, or fifteen years from now. You need a board, right now. Board members serve as advisers that in the short-term will, in simple terms, act as sanity checks and mentors. In the long-term, and conceivably, in some cases, after your departure as directors and representatives that act in the interest of your company.

You are putting in place a team that ensures that senior management and ownership interests are aligned. Now, if you do not have a board, don't fret you can do this once you adequately define the responsibilities of the board, identify some practices related to effective boards, and discuss some ways you can obtain board members for your company. Let's get started.

Now there are a bundle of economic theories that bring forward the business and economic rationale and need for a board. The crux of the debate is that ownership interests and managerial interests often are not aligned, And that managers need to be incentivized, rewarded, and monitored to ensure that they work in the best interests of the owner(s). This, in a very simplified view, is the foundation of agency theory. With this serving as the anchor, we have the traditional role of governance, which over time has expanded in scope and applies to your business just as much as it does to a Fortune 500 company. That is the board serves as a committee of professionals that is instrumental in setting the strategic direction of your company and ensure that your managers and employees are ethically and socially responsible.

Now that you have the theory, let's get to some practical insights and some executable actions. You will, likely in the early stages of your business, hand-select your board members based on personal relationships. That is find and encouraged, but it's important to note that your company board members need not be your best friends. They do need to be experienced business professionals and leaders. but business professionals and leaders that you know and trust. The reason for this is because the responsibilities of the board are important and will only increase in importance as your business grows. Here is another big reason, which may come as a surprise to you: a board member's loyalty is not to you as an individual, it's to your company.

You read that right. The board members' loyalty is to the company. Now in reality (and more than likely), your board members starting out will serve as mentors and guides to you; however, you must remember that as your company scales so does the true purpose of a board. In fact, your board members will not report to you. Now, you will hear some exceptions to this rule. Many of you may have heard how much influence Steve Jobs exerted over the board members of Apple; however, this is not normally the case, nor should you try to necessarily model that approach. Think of your board in its future state. The roles that your board members may perform range from helping to craft strategy, mission, and vision, overseeing implementation of strategy, gauging the perception of your business in the community, developing and enforcing ethics and social responsibility, and helping to identify potential opportunities and threats.

The depth of the role in the beginning is up to you, but it's important to remember that you need qualified board members that are straightforward, vetted, and honest with you regarding your business's direction. As you can likely discern, the implications of having an ethical board with defined roles is very important. Your board members are not there to perform your duties or that of other senior managers in your company; however, there are there to provide objective insight into the strategic direction of your company, observe its performance, and deliver recommendations that will contribute to its growth and profitability.

Now, let's get into the make-up of a board member. Your board members need to possess skills and knowledge that you lack, ideally coupled with considerable experience in business. Let me share an anecdote with you to give you some idea of how you may come into finding individuals with such skills. When I first started my company, I spoke to several individuals whom I thought could provide me insight in certain markets. Many of these professionals owned complementary businesses or were former managers within my network. There were a couple of instances where partnerships (filling capability gaps) were not in the interest of either party; however, there was enough interest in the company and a sense of loyalty to me where these people agreed to serve as board members. Some professional backgrounds of professionals considered for board positions included former senior military officers and civilian military leaders as well as community leaders. These leaders agreed to provide me with insight and perspective that would help grow the company, yet claimed loyalty to the company despite having a personal relationship with me.

This brings us to another key attribute of board members. Your board members need experience in areas that you currently lack consistent with your business strategy. As an example, your company may coordinate events for politicians, entertainers, and high-earning business professionals. You've defined your niche and know the target; however, you may be lacking a rolodex that's thick enough to get you started, or perhaps, you need expertise in how to garner repeat business within a high-end event planning business. Filling these gaps with individuals that possess experience in these areas will help you grow your business and provide insight you do not currently possess.

Now with this attention on skills, knowledge, and experience, there are some structural issues, individual attributes, and personality types that you want to avoid. Let's cover this and follow with an axiom I strongly buy-into based on my experiences as both business owner and adviser. First, make your board size manageable. Work to have a good mix of individuals and recognize that you will fill one of the positions on the board. If you have more than one owner, then consider a plus-one structure. A plus-one structure means that for every founder that will serve as a board member then add another founder who is not. As a general guide, a startup board makeup should consist of 5-to-7 members. This decision is yours; however, it is important to recognize when you have enough. I recommend that no more than seven board members serve on your company's board.

It's also important to recognize that in the beginning, this is your company and your vision. Of course, there will be people that help you along the way, and there will come a time when your current vision will be replaced with a more inclusive vision, yet in the beginning, it is yours. Having written this, you will have some board members that will be investors, some who will have experiences within the industry of your organization, and some members that possess specialized skills. Your investors will tend to want to exert some form of informal control, and the reality is that some of you will yield this control in favor of dollars. Just recognize that when you bring in investors as board members, especially venture capitalists, you will likely yield some control. Know just what you are yielding before bringing on investors as board members. Also, when you bring in industry experts, make role expectations known. What I have seen is that industry veterans are accustomed to being in charge and have the personality types to match. Be careful of these type of board members because it is not uncommon for them to meddle into the daily actions and activities of your company instead of staying focused on the strategic outcomes and long-term viability.

Mentioning all of these factors, you now have a focused and manageable range of considerations for when you select your board members. With these considerations, there is an important point to remember: You will have a mix of personalities, talents, knowledge, and skills on your board. You may have members who are also investors; you may have members that are former chief executives and some who are mentors and mangers. All of these professionals, ideally, provide your company with a healthy mix of skills and personalities that will be instrumental to growing and advancing your business aims. Yet, there is one thing that is not negotiable, and that is value alignment. Your company's board members' values must align with your company's values. This is important because board members are going to work to ensure that your company values are advanced during your tenure – and in some cases, after you leave. Board members will help you in ensuring that organizational roles are set, business values are clear, and create a sound governance structure that remains long after your departure. In addition, your company's board members will be instrumental in ensuring that the culture of your company is consistent with its values.

The next step is for you to develop what you need in your board members. Write-down five to seven individuals that can possible serve on your board.

Within the other headings (i.e., skills, knowledge, experience, and capital), write in a bullet format what the potential board member is bringing to the table. Don't skimp out in this area. Approach this section with rigor and put serious though into who can possibly serve on your company's board – envision what your board will look like. This is not a static representation, and you will revisit; however, for now, take some time to develop an initial (and ideal) board composition.

Activity 7 – Name that Board

Name	Skills	Knowledge	Experience	Capital
B1:				
B2:				
B3:				
B4				
B5:				
B6:				
B7:				

Now that you have some faces within the places, let's take a moment to define the roles. Outline the roles that you want your board members to perform from the list above:

Activity 8 – Board Role

Strategic Planning	Capital (Venture/ Non-Venture)	Risk Planning
Report Review	Liaison with Stakeholders	Controls Review
Ethics/Compliance	Industry Expertise	Specialized Skills
Employee Management Systems	Transparency & Disclosure	Policies, Processes, and Procedures

Board Member	Role
B1	
B2	
B3	
B4	
B5	
B6	
B7	

Next, the board itself (beginning with you) needs to develop a value statement. The approach to the value statement here is to initiate a draft for review. The draft value statement can be the same as the business value statement, or it can be separate yet supportive of the company's value statement. I recommend that you and the board members develop a separate value statement to account for the synergy, duties, and roles of the board that will be provided to each other and your company.

Activity 9 – Board Value Statements

_____

_____

_____

_____

_____

_____

Congratulations. You have just outlined your company's initial board make-up and drafted a value statement for board member review and input. Please take a moment to review your current board member agreement within your business binder or within your files and incorporate the necessary elements from the exercises above after making contact with your potential board. Maintain this exercise so that your board can revisit until you have finalized the make-up of your board, and so there is shared understanding and buy-in, which should include a clear and accepted understanding of roles, duties, responsibilities, and expectations.

Summary

The primary objective of this chapter was for you to reflect and develop a core set of values and ethics. Your work in this chapter brought forward the internal spiritual-based value system. With the business statements from Chapter One serving as the foundation, you were able to further develop your personal values and ethics that are aligned to your spiritual self. Next, you had an opportunity to develop a list of values, traits and behaviors sought for in your company board members. You discovered the importance of addressing skill-gaps while also recognizing that though there can be a gap in skills, that there can be no gap in values or ethics. There may be different internalizations yet the values and ethics should be shared. This reflection and the accompanying exercises helped you to build upon your spiritually-based strategy that extends your business to an enduring spiritual purpose and legacy.

CHAPTER 3

What's Going On and What Should We Do?

Wherefore we labour, that, whether present or absent, we may be accepted of him - 2 Corinthians 5:9 (KJV)

In Chapter One, you took a moment to reset. Specifically, you took a moment to reflect on your spiritual purpose. You reflected on how this connection extended to your business. You reflected on what your business stood for, above and beyond profit, and how your business connected with its key stakeholders. In Chapter Two, you conducted visioning exercises, which included reviewing and developing a vision and mission statement, as well as reviewing, developing, and reflecting on your business values. All of this connected with your personal core values initially developed and addressed in Chapter One. Next, you put forth considerable thought into the role your business plays in society and your community. This was followed by developing a governance framework that included developing (or refining) your company's board composition, the expected role of the board members, and developing a draft value statement for board members to consider and finalize. All of this work is important for your board is instrumental in helping you to oversee the strategic direction of your business and its commitment to the business and individual employee ethics and social responsibility.

That's a lot of ground covered in such a short time.

Now, you will take this spiritually-based framework and set some objectives and goals for your business. You may already have some goals and objectives developed (most of you likely do), but I am willing to bet that these lack the benefit of being grounded within a spiritual framework, and that many of you have a *strategic* set of objectives that are primarily operational and reactive in nature. When you first opened your business, this was likely enough. The strategic goals and objectives in the early going, in my experience, are operational in nature and scope. Achieving these goals and objectives may have even kept the lights on; however, now the aim is to have true strategic and operational goals and objectives. The strategic goals focus on growth and profitability, while also capturing what the business aims to achieve and its purpose above and beyond profit.

Within this spiritually-based framework, you will begin charting these objectives and goals, or as we would say in the Navy, *set course and speed*. Your course can be thought of as your business long-term objectives. This course has a destination, which is attainment of your business vision, and thereby requires concrete actions. The output here will serve as input to your company's short-term objectives and actions; the two shall meet and align.

Let's get started…

> ***Trust in the Lord with all thine heart; and lean not unto thine own understanding. In all thy ways acknowledge Him, and He shall direct thy paths*** - Proverbs 3:5-6 (KJV)

Long-term planning is not new. We can see it as far back as Noah, preparing for the great flood that drove him to build the ark. Advancing forward, we see Jesus preparing the disciples to carry forth His deeds and words. We see the value of long-term planning in armies and other forms of early organizations. Long-term planning, accompanied by objectives, is indeed associated with long-standing organizations. Why should your organization be any different?

You start this planning by asking just what path is needed to reach your business goals. Let's set forth an example. You may have a pizza parlor located downtown. Your pizza parlor is in its third year of business, and you notice that you are averaging about 5% growth in sales per year. You hear anecdotal information from your customers. They love the shop but wish you had more choices beside the standard pepperoni, sausage, combination, and other standard fares. You think about this and decide to form an informal meeting with your customers. You find out that most want different sizes of pizza, and some want pizza toast or breadsticks that taste like your crust. You find yourself considering both related products (miniature pizza) and complimentary products (chicken wings). These are often referred to as vertical and horizontal strategies and if done right can prove valuable to reaching your business goals and objectives. The next task is for you to start developing your own vertical and horizontal strategies.

But before you even consider taking any action, it's necessary for you to assess factors that impact your business within and outside the business. These forces can look toward trends and patterns, and consider factors such as technology, customer preferences, capital, and employee considerations. Take thirty minutes to complete the exercise below. You will **write down** at least six forces and pressures that impact your business; I started you off with an example. Next, you will score each factor on a scale of 1 through 5 (with 5 being High Impact). The next column distinguishes if the factor is an internal or external factor. An *I* represents an internal factors, and an *E* represents an external factor. The last column is a second score that represents how fast your company should respond to the factor you've identified. As you can see in the example below, competitive offerings have a high business impact; it's external in nature, and it demands a quick response.

Activity 1 - Business Forces and Pressures Impact Grid

Factor	Business Impact (1 – 5/5 = High Impact	Internal or External (I or E)	Response Score (1 – 5/5 = Quick Response	Total Score
Competitor Offerings	5	E	5	10

Once you have completed this activity, review your individually assigned scores. Factors with the highest scores warrant your immediate attention. From an intuitive perspective, high response scores would yield high business impact. Such scores likely indicate disruptive actions, that should be considered your *do now* or responsive actions. If you have this combination, the factor is likely transactional in nature and contributes to the survival of your business. Forces with a high Business Impact score and a low Response score are likely growth and/or profit-oriented factors.

In order to get to a point of strategic, spiritual development and execution, you must ensure that you address those short-term factors that threaten your business existence; you have to take care of the chaos, so that you can focus on your long-term growth and profitability. As you stabilize, you are going to then focus on the strategic factors that contribute to your company's long-term growth and profitability. So, here, your focus is two-fold. First, your business has to survive, so items that require a quick response and have a high impact receive your immediate attention. The actions out-flowing from this area will send you and your team in a flurry of activity – focused activity. Next, your goal is to redirect actions from survival to strategic. Think of this as an initial analysis that will link to your business statements and drive your specific business strategy.

Next, you need to take a look at your capabilities. Here you determine your resources and capabilities, along with your competencies. Some examples of resources and capabilities may include a highly skilled workforce, or an exceptional ability to generate new products faster than the competition. Your core competencies keep you honest and assess your company's capabilities against competitors. For example, you may have an ability to innovate; however, innovation for innovation's sake may lead to unrelated products reaching the market. But when you hold your core competencies that outflow from your business statements, then alignment is achieved. Do this now. Take a moment to enter two to four resources capabilities, and core competency items. Next, determine what core competency the entries align with in the table below; I provided two examples to help you get started.

Activity 2 – Resources, Capabilities, Core Competencies, and Alignment

Resources / Capabilities	Core Competency	Aligned (Y/N)
Skilled Workforce	Empowered and Motivated Workforce	Yes
Low Cost Structure	Delivered products lower than competitors with identical quality	Yes

You have now taken a look at your factors, as well as your resources/ capabilities, core competencies and made a determination (at least an initial determination) on the alignment of those business elements. The next step is to revisit the external and internal factors that have a high impact and/ or require a quick response and assess that alongside your resources and capabilities so that you can determine and frame the direction of your company.

Activity 3 – Forces/Pressures and RCC Assessment Charting

Factor	BI/RS Score	Resources / Capabilities	Core Competency	Aligned

Summary

You now have a snapshot of the direction your company is heading. The direction is aligned to the mission and vision statements you developed, consistent with your company values and ethics, and supportive of your company's social responsibility aims – and most importantly, all embedded with a spiritually-based framework. You have established these external and internal factors based on systematic analysis of the factors, resources, capabilities, and competencies that support your company's strategic aims and considered your company values and ethics. This is coupled with the benefit of what you can reasonably respond to, right now, based on your resources and capabilities. You should be getting real excited about your business yet there is still much work to do, so let's keep plugging away.

CHAPTER 4

Determine Course, Speed, and Direction

Commit thy works unto the LORD, and they thoughts shall be established - Job 22:21 (KJV)

When I was in the Navy, I obtained a qualification called Officer-of-the-Deck, which is basically someone qualified to navigate the ship and is responsible (next to the captain) for the ship's routine operation. One task that I was responsible for was determining the projected direction of the ship based on a pre-determined destination. A review of the forces and conditions that would impact the route toward the destination was already conducted; now, a general direction needed to be set. That is an appropriate analogy for where we are now. You are aware of the forces and factors that are impacting your business. You are also aware of your company's capabilities and areas of expertise and how this aligns with your strategic aims; now, we need to set course and speed. The way to do this is to set some long-range objectives supplemented by specific action plans that facilitate your target destination.

Take a moment to review your Forces/Pressures and RCC Assessment Chart. Do you notice any themes or patterns? Let's use an example: if a company is seeking only to sell chicken meals but also wants to expand into nuggets and chicken strips, this is often considered a product concentration strategy – chicken everything. In contrast, if a company is a small computer store that sells refurbished computers, then it may want to go into the supply process and make computer casings, which would lower its supply cost over time and allow it to achieve economies of scale. This is generally considered a vertical integrated strategy. Other approaches may consist of buying smaller competitors, forming alliances, or forming a joint venture to expand your company's service or product offering, while sharing the cost of production, development, marketing, and delivery. The point is that if you look closely, a theme or series of themes appear that you need to classify so that you can frame some long-term objectives.

Before launching into specific long-term strategies, we need to ensure certain principles related to business success are clear. There is a famous axiom that states that the lifeblood of a business is cash-flow. That, in my experience, is true. Without cash-flow that results from the sale of YOUR company products and services, there is really not much of a business to worry about. The business ideally is positioned to achieve profit, which is a key objective and intent of the firm. So having cash-flow and profit as key considerations – better yet as obligations of the business to its owners and other key stakeholders, you can begin to consider specific methods and strategies that meet those objectives. The good thing is that many of you have an infrastructure on which to meet those two core objectives. The challenge is identifying the means in which these challenges will be addressed.

Using the pizza shop example earlier, there are a few ways one can grow the pizza shop. These different approaches are called strategies. Think of how your actual business, and other businesses, earn profits. One strategy approach could be product concentration (making different variants of a single product). Another strategy approach could be a concentrated growth strategy (expanding the reach of a business by offering similar or complimentary products). There are of course other approaches at the other end of the spectrum. For example, GE competes in several markets and has multiple products lines and services. This strategy is often referred to as a diversified strategy (unrelated) and is pursued by conglomerates (companies that compete in multiple industries and markets). Just as there are multiple strategic approaches, there are multiple ways to classify the general strategic direction of your company; however, for our purposes, we are going to keep these simple.

First, you are operating on a few dimensions right now. You can be operating on the basis of price, or you could be competing on the basis of providing a commodity service in a very unique way. As an example, a company may serve the best burgers in the neighborhood based on a sauce that's been in the family for years at a reasonable (and attractive) price point. Another company may cater to a special group of clients. For example, it may provide security services for small businesses located within retail shopping centers. These are the only clients the business serves, and it has developed a level of expertise and specialized services that meets (and in some cases, exceeds) their needs. These are all strategies, and we need to reflect on classifying these approaches for your business right now.

Activity 1 – Classifying My Small Business Strategy

Priced-Based: These are strategies pursued by small companies that are going to generate sales, revenue, and profits primarily by competing on the basis of price.

Niche-Based: These are strategies pursued by small companies whose approaches are centered on fulfilling the needs of certain clients within a specific industry or market.

Capabilities, Features, and Functions-Based: These are strategies that are pursued by small businesses whose current approaches are centered on providing distinctive capabilities, features, and functions related to product offering.

Having examined these three strategies, let's determine your primary classification by completing the following:

My small business is primarily _____
_-based. This is based on our products (or service) that provides
_____ (name the product or service) to

43

_____ (identify the customer or client) who expect (name the attributes your customer/client is seeking).

Take a few moments to reflect on the statement above, WHILE reviewing your organizational statements and charts. What are some insights that you gained based on this review? Please note these in four-five sentences below:

_____

_____

_____

_____

_____

_____

Now that you have some indication of your generalized approach to pursuing your business strategy, let's take a look at underlying support strategies, first by classifying these strategies, and then by determining your approach. These strategies are important because they are essentially connected to your general strategy – a strategy within a strategy.

If we take the pizza restaurant example, the company may seek to make variants of pizza or provide other dishes. If the owner decides to expand the product line by offering more pizza products, this is referred to, for our purposes, as a **directed-related strategy**. Pizza is everything. You remember that movie *Forest Gump* and how Forest's friend talked about shrimp? The same thing holds here. The owner may sell mini-pizzas, pizzas-on-the-run, pizza strips, everything pizza. These direct-related strategies are all in common.

In a similar yet different approach, the owner may work to develop complimentary products. Pizza and wings; pizza and tacos; pizza, wings, and tacos – these are considered complimentary items and for our purposes, are called **directed-unrelated strategy**. The way to think about this is that we are maintaining the flagship products (pizza), yet we are expanding the product offering by providing complimentary products.

Another strategy that you may pursue is providing products and services to the market quicker than your competitors. Apple's rush of consumer-based technology products is an example. Its inventions from the iPod to iPhone were quick well-time introductions in which Apple self-cannibalized itself. Your company may pursue a similar approach. You may have provided, as a simple example, digital photographic services that produced a slideshow on a disk. Now, you provide video services via social media that are accompanied by a slideshow that can be made available by accessing company-owned servers 24/7 by your clients. For our purposes this is called a **product/service-innovation strategy**.

Your next move may be to leverage economies of scale by producing the products and material that go into your product or expanding downstream by becoming our own distributor. An example is that our pizza shop owner decides that his crust is better than the competitors and has found a way to increase production, while lowering costs to a point where it is both efficient and of the desired quality he seeks. His customers love it. For our purposes, this is called a **stretch strategy**, so named because, in this example, the company is stretching across the supply or the distribution end of her company.

As another example, maybe our pizza restaurant owner wants to tap into a related market at a different income segment. With cash on hand, the owner decides to purchase space for a high-end eatery that specializes in pizzas. This location is in a suburban area where the average income is $120,000. The owner knows that offering a fine dine-in experience will enable her to increase her margins and gain space in that market. She is also able to expand her reach without contaminating her core brand. For our purposes, these are **breadth strategies** where the owner is essentially acquiring, developing, or expanding an existing brand, branching into new markets or area.

Activity 2 – Classifying My Small Business Strategy (Part II)

With these underlying support strategies in place, it's time for us to identify or clarify the underlying strategy for your business. Let's start by revisiting the generalized strategy statement made above:

My small business is primarily _____
_-based. This is based on our products (or service) that provides _____ (name the product or service) to _____ (identify the customer or client) who expect _____ (name the attributes your customer/client is seeking).

We will now add the underlying strategy. Please take twenty minutes to complete the second element of this activity.

Based on the generalized strategy, the underlying strategy is determined to be _____. This is based on the company's effort to achieve increased growth and profitability by _____
_____
_____.

When these elements are combined, you have outlined your primary business strategy – isn't that neat?! However, we need to take the time to make this a cohesive element of your business plan. So let's summarize.

Activity 3 – Integrating Core Capabilities, Generalized Strategy, and Underlying Strategy

My company's core capabilities are: _____

_____

_____.

These core capabilities are essential to my small business that is primarily _____-based. This is based on our product (or

service) that provides _____ (name the product
or service) to _____ (identify the customer
or client) who expect _____ (name the attributes
your customer/client is seeking).

Based on the above generalized strategy, the underlying strategy is
determined to be _____. This is based
on the company's effort to achieve increased growth and profitability by:
_____ its products and services.

Summary

The primary objective of this chapter was for you to consider the general
strategic direction of your company based on your spiritually-based business
statements, values and ethics, and assessment of forces and pressures. As
shared earlier, it's not that this is so much new, yet what is unique is the
spiritually-based approach that will yield a sustainable culture focused on
equity, justice, and fair treatment. This was a big step for two reasons. First,
you have taken the first step to make your spiritually-based framework
real. Second, you are about to embark into specific actions that will result
in measurable behaviors that set the stage for owner, manager, employee,
and customer interactions. Your customers will intuitively know that your
business is operating from a spiritual core. It may or may not be expressed
yet it will be perceived and felt. It will be real.

CHAPTER 5

Looking Again at our Customers

Have not I commanded thee? Be strong and of a good courage;
be not afraid neither be dismayed, for the Lord thy God is
with thee whithersoever thou goest – Joshua 1:9 (KJV)

Knowing who your customer is and defining, predicting, and responding to their needs can enable your company to deliver on, and at times, exceed your customer's expectations. Many entrepreneurs consider the aforementioned processes to be solely in the realm of marketing. Yet, knowing how you will compete in your industry, the signal that you send to your customers and understanding their needs, and introducing new products and services –or at the very least, finding better ways to deliver on existing needs, is an all-hands effort that is inclusive of, yet extends beyond marketing.

As every man hath received the gift, even so minister
the same one to another, as good stewards of the
manifold grace of God – 1 Peter 4:10 (KJV)

After having written this, now is the time to reflect on who you are serving: just who are your customers? Once you answer this, you can think of more effective ways to serve those customers. You know where they are. You can predict when their demand will fluctuate. You will know what products and services to add to your portfolio. You know what they value and what they expect, and your employees will work to ensure that that these expectations are met each and every time. Knowing this bundle of expectations and how to deliver it is an *all-hands-on-deck effort.*

And it's important for...

Every business has competitors. Some of these competitors are direct, and some are indirect, yet for the most part, we all have some competition. One of the things that makes me cringe is when I see a new entrepreneur say, "There is nothing like this on the market," or "We are the first company to offer the service this way." While that may be true – and it can be true - there is someone that has the capability to offer what you offer, or who will respond to your product or service offerings at some point. The company that does this may be in the same industry; perhaps, they have the same capabilities; or perhaps, they served you in the early days and want to experience similar success. So instead of obsessing about being the first and only, I tell business owners to focus on being the best they can be in a contested space. What does that mean? That means winning. That means being number one or number two, or owning a space where your brand stands-out, and we are going to go through that process... right now.

Activity 1 – Who is Out There – Part I

Your next step is to define that space. To clarify where you need to be – or where you are trying to be. Take a moment to write down five competitors. If you have that special one-of-a-kind product and in your mind, that no one else even comes close, then look to your industry and write down five competitors that come as close to your product or service. Let's get started.

My company's five competitors are as follows:

C1: _____

C2: _____

C3: _____

C4: _____

C5: _____

Now these are the firms that you can expect to respond efficiently to your company's product and service offerings. What is an efficient response? Well that depends, but at the very least, we are going to estimate that within the next year some type of response will occur. Why are they going to respond? These reasons can vary. *You have my share of customers* (turf). You may have identified a sweet spot that is attractive to competitors. Perhaps, the segment is so underserved that the competition views that it can fill the void and gap. It may be a bundle of all these factors… and more. The point is this: your competition is not going to just stand around and watch – and that, if you don't know already, can be a good thing. Take a moment to reflect and think of the response that you can expect.

_____

_____

_____

_____

_____

_____

The next step is to write down the similar products or services that your competitors provide and assign a score. Let's start first with writing down similar products or services from your competitors.

C1 (products and services):_____

_____

C2 (products and services): _____

_____

C3 (products and services): _____

_____

C4 (products and services): _____

_____

C5 (products and services): _____

_____

The next step is to rank these competitors based on the similarity of experience that your customers may experience in terms of product functionality or continuity of service. The more similar the benefits and features, the stronger the degree of competition. Take a moment to review and reflect on your above assessment and re-rank your competitors based on the degree of similarity.

My company's five competitors (**re-ranked**) are as follows:

C1:_____

_____

C2: _____

_____

C3: _____

_____

C4: _____

_____

C5: _____

_____

Your next step is to do a form of forecasting. I will start now by stating two things. First, forecasting is not easy. Second, forecasting is not perfect. It's akin to hearing the weather professional on the news say there is a 50% chance of showers. In simple terms, it's the probability that something will occur, but is no guarantee that it will occur. When it comes to your competitors, you don't know everything about their financial state, their commitments, or the degree to which the customer is willing to switch. Yet, you do have information.

You may have access to information, and you will employ that information to increase the reliability of your forecast. You will use this information to help you develop contingency plans for actions executed or risk mitigation planning for proposed actions that emerge within your company's business environment. So, with this overview, let's take a moment to write down a response that you can expect from each competitor based on your company's actions – such as the introduction of products and services that your company provides. In completing this element, you will need other sources of information. Some information sources that you may use include information from press/media, company's public statements, websites, trade reports, trade conferences, or even based on anecdotal information you have heard from other customers. Hopefully, you will revisit this section as you progress through the lessons and activities, and as your business advances.

Let's get started.

Take a moment to forecast your competitors' responses below.

C1 (Response): _____

_____

C2 (Response): _____

_____

C3 (Response): _____

_____

C4 (Response): _____

_____

C5 (Response): _____

_____

As you can probably note, there is considerable *noise* even for unique products and services; however, you will be prepared. One way to be prepared starts with knowing where you stand in relation to your competition. The next step is to revisit your customers. This will be done by "going back to the basics," which you will find is often just what is needed in a fast-paced and often, chaotic business environment. You will look once again at just who is your customer. You will also look at how they live, consider their beliefs and opinions, know their income levels, and be familiar with their behaviors. You will know what they look like from a demographic perspective (race, age, gender, etc.) and what they believe, and what interests that have (psychographics). Why is this important? Because knowing this allows you to more effectively deliver on what they expect from your company. It helps enable you to more efficiently and effectively employ resources. It helps you create a compelling message that is consistent with your spiritually-based company and individual and business values. It's a big deal.

Let's get started.

Based on the information you have available and your research, what area(s) do your customers live?

My customers live in _____.

Based on the information you have available and your research, what are the values, perspectives, income, and views of your customers?

My customers value _____.

My customers' views and perspectives are _____

_____.

My customers' opinions and perspectives are _____

_____

_____

My customers' income level ranges from _____ to _____.

Based on the information you have available and your research, what do your customers look like? Are they young, old, black, white, Hispanic, Asian? Do you have customers that are gay or bi-sexual? These are questions that are important and provide you an indication of your core. What's important to understand is that you are not indicating or signaling that your business is not inclusive. It's that these are the factors that best describe and capture your target market and match your customer profile. So having this as the backdrop, let's go to the next step and get busy describing your primary customer demographic.

My customers are _____

_____.

Since this is a series geared toward existing business owners and senior leaders within young companies, I am assuming that at this point in your business stage of growth, you have spoken with customers, examined data related to your competitors (in the past, as well as information needed to get to this point in the series), and know at some level, where your customers live, their values, their beliefs, what they look like, and what they want. Now you need to revisit what your business means to your customers by reflecting on the above competitor and customer information in the aggregate.

Now, this segmentation, targeting, and competitive actions are not unique; however, the spiritually-based approach is distinctive. You are basing your company on spiritual principles. So in addition to reviewing the competitor and customer profiles above, you will also need to bring forward your spiritual statements, along with your vision, mission, the other organizational statements you've developed. All of this must align with who you are and where your business is heading. Based on this holistic assessment, you can now refine your product and service offering. So the final step in this section is to gain clarity on your customer needs and expectations. You will answer this by assessing what your customers expect your company "to be," "to provide," "to do," "to guarantee," "to respect," and the problem or need that "needs to be solved."

Activity 2 – Delivering on Expectations

My customers expect my company to:

_____

_____

_____

_____

_____

All while being led by spiritually-based leaders who understand the purpose of a business beyond profit.

Activity 3 – Play It Again, Sam

Your final task is to bring all the activities together to tie-in our customers and acknowledge our competitors in a more refined and specific way. Let's get going.

Based on the generalized strategy, the underlying strategy is determined to be _____. This is based on the company's effort to achieve increased growth and profitability by _____

_____

_____its products and services.

My company's core capabilities are: _____

_____

_____.

These core capabilities are essential to my small business and are primarily _____-based. This is based on our product (or service) that provides _____ (name the product or service) to _____ (identify the customer or client).

Our competition consists of five companies. These five competitors are:

_____

_____

_____.

Expected responses include:

_____

_____

_____.

Our customers live in _____.
These customers value _____ and
hold an opinion that our company should_____. The
customers buy when _____.
Our customers expect for our products and services to include
_____ (name the attributes your
customer/client is seeking).

Later, as you develop what are typically considered functional processes, you will have an opportunity to define how you will reach your customers. You will also have an opportunity to develop and reflect on price points, and consider the ways in which your customer will gain access to your project and service. These elements are also generally related to marketing functions. For now, you have broadly outlined just who these customers are, what other companies also service these customers, and how you plan to reach these customers, while also preparing for a response from your competitors.

Summary

In this chapter, you addressed the course, speed, and direction of your business. Specifically, you assessed the forces that were revealed in Chapter 3 and assessed these against your company's core competencies. Based on that information, you developed a generalized strategy. These strategies included price-based; niche-based; and capabilities, features, and function-based strategies. Upon assigning your business to a generalized strategy, we discussed and assigned your business to an underlying strategy. These strategies included director-related; director-unrelated; product/service innovation, stretch, and breadth. Next, you combined your business core competencies with the generalized and specific strategies that resulted in a business model. Finally, you took a look at your competitors and customers, assessing the capabilities and commitment of the competition by asking what the customer wants or expects. You then revisited all these areas that resulted in customer and competitor profiles. These profiles enable you to sharpen your company's capabilities, and product and service offerings.

CHAPTER 6

Acting on the Planning

Be ye strong therefore, and let not your hands be weak: for your work shall be rewarded – 2 Chronicles 15:7 (KJV)

Next to not having a plan, in my experience, the second biggest thing holding entrepreneurs and business owners back from obtaining successful growth and profitability is an inability to execute on the elements within their business plan. Most of this is largely due to the plans not having concrete or measurable actions with specific targets and criteria for success. When I probe into the reasoning for entrepreneurs and business owners lack of planning, it generally comes down to inexperience or not taking the time to define specific actions that lead to the achievement of the business vision.

It's amazing that as standard and important as business plans are, the banks and non-profits that help many businesses acquire funding rarely look for concrete actions. In fact, the only thing you really notice that is done with any rigor is the pro forma projections generally inherent within this plan. Now, don't get me wrong. There are some concrete start-up plans out there, and these plans are quite impressive; however, in reality, this is rarely the case. Unless your business has some concrete plans that are measurable with specific targets, in my view, you really don't have a plan. Instead, you have a generalized list of objectives and possibilities, but you really do not have a business plan. So now that we discussed the problem, let's get down to some specifics and outline concrete actions, goals, and milestones for your business's next stage of growth.

You remember our pizza restaurant owner? She had a couple of options available to her, and we fit these into examples that included **breadth strategies** and **depth strategies** as examples. In that example, those were the underlying strategies that linked to the business owner's **generalized strategies**. Now within those underlying strategies are some specific objectives and goals that are measured over a period of time.

Long-term goals, for example, may include introducing three new products within the next three years. This long-term goal is essentially one new pizza or related complimentary product per year, which is aggressive, yet the owner feels is doable. Another goal may be to increase profits by twenty percent over the next three years. This is another big goal that requires a specific, concrete action plan.

So what may these actions look like to you? Well in the case of the new product introduction, this could include administering survey forms to customers via websites and in-store locations. Questions within the survey may focus on type of products the customers would like to see added to the menu. This could also include doing a new one-time special once a quarter to gain insight into "likeability" or sales during the special period or on a limited time product. Finally, this could include something as simple as a bonus for an employee that develops an idea for a new product and helps coordinate the trial period introduction.

Back to the pizza shop example, related to the owner's second goal, which was to increase profits by twenty percent over the next three years, several concrete actions may occur. One could be an effort to reduce waste. The restaurant owner could pass a small incentive to employees (perhaps a share of the savings) that have an accurate cash drawer, "till," or who use a prescribed allowance of products (i.e. napkins, ketchup, and other condiments) during a thirty-day period. Now with this waste reduction (equating to cost reduction), the owner also recognizes that there are some investments in growth profitability areas needed, so she increases advertising within local publications that target her market. She also enhances her restaurant to accommodate more traffic that meets her customers' requests for more open space – additional insight she gained from her survey. She may also find floor space that provides additional sales opportunities.

These actions, if well-managed and executed, could contribute to increased profits while also improving customer loyalty and job satisfaction. Now is the time to provide some disclaimers. Refining your business's long-term objectives and selecting the right short-term objectives and actions is not an easy process, and it will require you to be able to discern and learn quickly.

Having said this, let's get started with some preliminary planning. Let's start with targeting long-term objectives. Your company's long-term objectives will likely be achieved three to five years from the moment you begin to execute actions toward their achievement. These objectives need to be challenging yet realistic. Concrete yet also flexible (see examples above). The next step is to get started and re-focus (or provide initial focus) to specific objectives for your business.

Activity 1

Please take a moment to write down three to five long-term objectives for your business:

O1: _____

O2: _____

O3: _____

O4: _____

O5: _____

Now take a moment to ensure that these objectives are in alignment with your spiritually-based business planning thus far. Review your spiritual statements – rate each objective on a scale of 1 (weak alignment) to 5 (strong alignment) – please assign only whole numbers. Any long-term objective listed that is scored below three needs to be revisited and should be placed as a low- priority objective if it maintains that score. Next, you will need to rank each objective. For example, you may have two "5"s and two "4"s; however, you are limited by resources (time, money, personnel, etc.). As a result, your next step is to prioritize your high-ranked long-term objectives. Now let's slate this list:

Activity 2

Please take a moment to re-slate your top long-term objectives that are not prioritized based on (a) alignment and (b) resources and constraints:

Q1: _____

Q2: _____

Q3: _____

Q4: _____

Q5: _____

With these long-term objectives come specific actions that must occur, your concrete daily actions. You will now focus on these specific actions. Keep in mind that these actions must be measured and have accompanying targets. You cannot merely state the action. You need to define "success" and ensure that the measurements are realistic and consistent with the organizational goals you developed.

When developing your short-term objectives, there are several things you need to keep in mind:

Number One: These actions should be completed within one year.

Number Two: Linkage of daily, short-term actions is not an option. If the action does not link to the long-term objective, then it should not be considered or pursued. It's that simple.

Number Three: These actions serve as input to your policies and action plans. Use the actions you developed as source material for company policies to ensure that you and your employees' actions are consistent with the mission and vision.

Number Four: The identified short-term actions provide points of accountability and responsibility. The identified objectives should be developed for immediate and future applicability, while recognizing that these points of accountability and responsibility are also captured in policy, operating procedures, and action plans.

Number Five: Look for points of tension between your action plans. If there is some tension or conflict within the action plans, you and your team should assess the selected strategies to serve as the overarching guide for making decisions.

Let's go through a few examples of what these may look like in motion. Remember the body shop owner? Well, her business is tracking in its third year, and her profits are averaging $150,000 per year. She feels comfortable that her business can survive, and now is focused on opening an additional location (growth) to increase revenue and profitability. Our business owner feels she can achieve increased profitability by increasing volume. Her long-term goal is to increase shop earnings by fifteen percent in the next three years. This needs to be translated to specific short-term goals, which may include:

SA: To increase after-tax revenue by 5% in Year 1

SA: To increase shop orders by 3% in FQ-Year

SA: To increase complimentary sales (detailing) by 5% in Year 1

Notice how all the above examples are concrete, specific, measurable, and occur in a short-time frame. Also review and note how these actions align

With the owner's long-term objectives. With this example in mind, take your objectives listed on the previous page and develop one to three short-term objectives that support each long-range objective.

Activity 3

Q1: _____

    SA1: _____

    SA2: _____

    SA3: _____

Q2: _____

    SA1: _____

    SA2: _____

    SA3: _____

Q3: _____

    SA1: _____

    SA2: _____

    SA3: _____

Q4: _____

    SA1: _____

    SA2: _____

    SA3: _____

Q5: _____

    SA1: _____

    SA2: _____

    SA3: _____

As comprehensive as the listing of the short-term objectives was, you are not done yet. You must now look for priority and tension. Please take a minute to review the listing above and ensure that you rank the underlying short-term actions. If the actions are not listed in order, take a pencil and place the correct priority number under each objective to the right of the statement. The final step in this part of the exercise is to identify points of tension. An example of a point of tension is the body shop owner seeking to provide high quality paint services, while also selecting paint vendor/paint type based on price criteria. After you've identified points of tension, write the world "tension" and the conflicting short-term objective. For example, our body shop business owner may have a Q1/SA1 that reads: Reduce supply material costs by 5%, and a Q2/SA1 that reads: Ensure high-quality paint supplier procured from ISO-certified provider. It is reasonable to assume that these two objectives could possibly be at odds (reducing material cost for paint could be lower not higher in quality), so in this example you could mark that to the side of the objective of Q1/SA2 tension with Q1/SA1. After identification of tension points, take a moment to reflect and resolve how you will overcome this point of tension. In fact, let's do that now.

Activity 4 – Resolving the Tension

Where you have identified points of tension, take a moment to write down how you will resolve the tension for each identified point.

T1: _____

_____

T2: _____

_____

T3: _____

_____

T4: _____

_____

T5: _____

_____

Summary

Within this section, you revisited your strategies at all levels. This included reviewing your breadth and depth strategies and your generalized strategies. From that point, you developed some long-term objectives based on those strategies (strategic thrusts for you advanced business types). Next, you rated the long-term objectives and calculated a score to assess the strength of the alignment between your business strategies and your spiritual and organizational statements. Once you achieved alignment, short-terms objectives were developed along with specific actions needed to meet the short-term objectives you defined. The actions were then reassessed for alignment and assigned a desired level of performance proficiency (performance measure). The next step is to focus on some financial elements related to your business. Let's get started.

CHAPTER 7

Assessing Financial Health and Building Financial Capacity

But thou shalt remember the LORD thy God: for [it is] he that giveth thee power to get wealth, that he may establish his covenant which he sware unto thy fathers, as [it is] this day – Deuteronomy 8:18 (KJV)

Assessing the financial health and capacity of your business is one of the most important strategy planning actions that you will take. Monitoring your business health is one of your key responsibilities. Perhaps, one of the most disturbing things I see is business owners not being aware of their company's financial health. There are firms that are technically insolvent or lack the financial capacity to remain in operation over the course of the next year. These businesses are hoping and praying for a miracle. There are business hoping for a sudden influx of cash resulting from an external event, or perhaps an extension on a line-of-credit.

For your business to reach its next stage of growth, this cannot be the case, and it starts with knowing your current financial reality.

As a business owner, not knowing the financial health of your company from a short- and long-term perspective is not an option, and we are going to spend some time going over some basic financial information that can help you gauge the health of your business. So let's get started.

There are three key statements that you should have available in your business. These statements are as follows (Note: Don't have nightmares and don't say you don't like math; this is an important area, and take it from one business owner to another, intimate knowledge of its contents are absolutely critical):

Balance Sheet: In capturing the assets and liability of your company, the balance sheet's value is that it captures your company's financial health at a specific point in time. Practically speaking, the balance sheet can lead to some business owners thinking that their financial health is better than what's reported. There is a difference between forced balancing and having a firm grasp one your company's financial health. You need to be acutely aware what is convertible to cash in the short-term and those assets which are illiquid or not easily convertible to cash. You also need to be aware of the long-term debt and what's due in the short-term. In sum, the balance sheet is necessary, but it is not sufficient to solely gauge the health and financial viability of your company.

Income Statement: This is one of the most important statements that helps you to gage what's going on in your business because you or an observer can see all the asset and expense transactions that occurred for a specific period. In practice, this sheet is a great tool for you to assess the margin on your products and observe how costs are impacting your business income. From an owner's perspective, the income statement provides a reporting of net income and changes in owner's equity. Practically speaking, what I see is that owners and accountant professionals often have challenges in accurately recording expenses and revenue. As a business owner, you need to be aware of the generally accepted accounting principles (GAAP) in this area and ensure that your business transactions are accurately recorded. The income statement, from a projected perspective, is also a great tool to "plug and play" estimations to assess transactional-based decisions that impact margins.

Statement of Cash Flow: A quick rule of thumb for you to keep in mind is that cash flow statements show how cash is moved within your company. Your investors, bankers, and creditors generally grab this sheet in tandem with the income statement because it provides how cash flows in and out of your business. In addition, it distinguishes the source and purpose of the cash, providing insight between cash employed for operations, financing, and investing. Important for you and your team to know is how the contributions feed into the numbers. Practically speaking, the operations elements of your business are the elements that attract the attention of investors, creditors, and other potential sources of capital in determining the long-term health of your company. As someone who has consulted companies in turnaround situations, I am keenly focused on "adjustments to convert" to cash. In plain English, I am looking to know just how the company is collecting its receivables, the amount collected, and what's truly under control of the company. The statement of cash flow and balance sheet provide good insights into this conversation.

Forecasting Needs and Controlling Efforts

One of the most important strategic activities is forecasting the company's needs; yet, in practice, there are few young companies that do it, and those that do, apply a rear-view window approach that proves insufficient in developing sound forecasting requirements needed by the company. From a strategic planning perspective, you need to build a forecasting model that addresses the long-term financial business needs while also acknowledging its present condition. In addition, the output of your forecasting, the budget, helps to guide efforts that your company undertakes in pursuit of its strategy.

Forecasting and budgeting are absolutely essential to the strategic and operational success of your company. It is an area that I am particularly attuned to because I see so many business owners that do not know the cost of their activities. I see business owners whose businesses scale, and they have no way of knowing how efforts in one area of their business impact the other areas. Or, they are working from a non-classified budgeting process that does not provide a clear indicator of where and how financial resources are spent. Another source of resistance for forecasting and budgeting is because, quite simply, it's not easy. Unless you are "wired" to love painstaking processes that involve quantifying what may, at times, seem to be unquantifiable, then there is a good chance that you may not like the science of forecasting and budgeting.

On the other hand, there are companies that swing hard to the right. Where there are just too many actions tied to budgetary and financial controls. Where the remarks such as, "it's not in the budget" are used as disguises for not formulating sound plans and actions. Or where, common sense decisions are not made because of some obsessive adherence to a company's budget.

Let's take a moment to frame some foundational forecasting and budget philosophies and tools that you can build upon as you pursue the strategy and actions plans developed herein. What will become immediately evident, if effectively utilized, is how your financial tools and models can bring clarity and insight to the projects and programs that your business pursues. What will also become evident is how developing quantifiable measures that accompany or underlie budgeting can make vague actions, specific and concrete. Here is an important note that I am proud to bring forward. Most business strategy and entrepreneur start-up books are very vague in this area. That is because many authors are (1) not business owners; and (2) they lack the experience associated with business forecasting. As a result, their recommendations and suggestions are based in theory and not where financial forecasting actually occurs. You will not have that problem here for effective forecasting is an iterative process that starts, in your case, the moment you start to formulate short-term objectives and will continue down throughout the action planning of your business planning. So let's get started.

Activity 1: Forecasting to Long Range Requirements

In the above section, you articulated your short-term objectives based on your long-term objectives. Now take a moment to bring down the short-term objectives here and start to cost activities. Take a moment to write-down your business short-term objectives in the sections below. Next, you will write down activities that support the objectives and estimate the cost (Note: This is an iterative process, and you will revisit – ideally on a scheduled frequency basis):

Q1: _____

    SA1: _____

    SA2: _____

    SA3: _____

Actions/Tasks and Cost Estimate (Note: You will place your cost estimate in parentheses):

_____

_____

_____

Estimated Total Cost: _____

Q2: _____

    SA1: _____

    SA2: _____

    SA3: _____

Actions/Tasks and Cost Estimate (Note: You will place your cost estimate in parentheses):

_____

_____

_____

Estimated Total Cost: _____

Q3: _____

     SA1: _____

     SA2: _____

     SA3: _____

Actions/Tasks and Cost Estimate (Note: You will place your cost estimate in parentheses):

_____

_____

_____

Estimated Total Cost: _____

Q4: _____

     SA1: _____

     SA2: _____

     SA3: _____

Actions/Tasks and Cost Estimate (Note: You will place your cost estimate in parentheses):

_____

_____

_____

Estimated Total Cost: _____

Q5: _____

    SA1: _____

    SA2: _____

    SA3: _____

Actions/Tasks and Cost Estimate (Note: You will place your cost estimate in parentheses):

_____

_____

_____

Estimated Total Cost: _____

Once again, it's important to note that this is an iterative process, and you will revisit throughout your business planning cycles. You should be pleased with yourself. You have taken the first step of articulating forecasting and budget requirements that will serve you well.

Generating and Obtaining Funds for Growth

Earlier there was discussion on the *current reality* of your business. You captured strategic funding considerations based on your company's current financial position and capacity. Yet, your company's capacity will change. Ideally, if you're doing it right and over the long-term, your financial capacity will grow. However, I am assuming that most of you are at a stage in your company's growth cycle where every penny counts and where there never seems to be enough cash in the bank. In other words, your company's current reality makes the explicit consideration of raising capital and financing your business operations an important issue and consideration during the strategic planning and execution phases.

The most often discussed (and generally thought of) ways to raise capital for your business is through bank loans and friends. While the latter certainly is an option and not unusual, the chances that you are going to get the loan that you need to cover all your business financing, even in the short-term, is not realistic. Related to the latter, while your friends and family members are certainly an option, I can think of few ways that are faster in losing the favor of someone you value and love. Now that is not to say that you should take it "off the table," it certainly does carry with it considerable risk; however, it is not a viable strategic consideration to fund your business for the long-term. Below are some strategic considerations that your company may consider to finance its growth:

Venture Capital: Venture capital continues to be a viable funding source for startup and existing companies that are still early in their business lifecycles. Venture capital allows you, in a best-case scenario, to retain enough control to chart the future of your company. Yet, there are often some issues to consider when deciding to take on venture capital. First, the moment you take venture capitalist funds, you will give up some direction and control of your company. How much, of course, depends on the company, the amount of funding, and the terms and conditions of the deal. There are some good reasons for this, and venture capitalists have a good track record in investing in *winners*.

Licensing: Licensing is a viable option for some of you as business owners, especially those of you that introduce unique technology-based solutions or products. The decision to license brings with it some tangible benefits. First, in pursuing this strategy, you are generally going to focus on the solution (or process or product) while your licensees focus on the forward-facing strategies such as marketing, sales, operations, and manufacturing. Some of the benefits include sharing the cost of entering new markets and an accelerated ability to scale.

Passive Partners/Co-Owners: Taking on partners and co-owners are good strategies, so long as there is reasonable *skin in the game* for all interested parties. Of course, the more active the partner, the more impact this has on your business structure, and the more control you will likely have to yield. Common business structures include general and limited partnership, and limited liability companies, all of which have their upsides and downsides (Note: Please ensure you consult with your lawyer and accountant when considering a final business structure).

Summary

In this section, you engaged in some very important financial activities and reflected upon key financial issues that you may consider going forward. Specifically, you assessed the financial health of your business as it relates to its current reality. You reviewed the role of the balance sheet, income statement, and cash flow statement. Next, you brought forward your long-term forecasting requirements and aligned those with short-term activities and actions. Once you developed those actions and tasks, you estimated the cost of these actions to help frame your budget requirements. Finally, you reflected on ways that you may increase the capacity and reach, and ways you could possibly gain leverage through a brief consideration of the benefits of licensing, venture capital, and various form of partnership structures. An important note that bears repeating is this: please ensure you contact your lawyer or accountant for specific information on the financial activities and business structures discussed in this chapter. The intent here was for you to revisit from a strategic planning perspective and not to provide a prescriptive advice. See, it wasn't so bad. You covered some important ground, and you should be proud.

Let's keep going.

CHAPTER 8

Recognizing, Valuing, and Employing Human Capital

Let noting be done through strife or vainglory; but
in lowliness of mind let each esteem other better
than themselves – Philippians 2:3 (KJV)

One of the most common and biggest challenges faced by the entrepreneur is developing an initial workforce plan and conducting initial hiring. If I am lucky, I may find clients that have some broad plan that contains a few positions and the required (or desired) qualifications and experience for the developed position. Generally, however, this is not the case. And that's a problem. It a problem because hiring employees is going to be one of your biggest and most significant actions as a business owner, and you need a workforce plan before you open your doors, not when you find a sudden need to "get some help." Many business owners wrongfully assume that initial workforce planning needs to be elaborate and complicated; it doesn't. In fact, quite the opposite is what's needed, which is a simple plan that succinctly articulates your business workforce requirements. In this section, you are going to develop your initial plan; a plan that outlines your requirements by job position.

It is important for you to recognize this: jobs are important to your organization and to your employee. It is your company; however, the job, once filled, is an important part of your employee's identity. Your employees come to work for a variety of reasons. Some of it may be about you, especially in the beginning, yet it can also (and often is) be about the job itself. There may be a sense of passion that engages the employee to tasks related to the job; it may be the product or service that is provided to the end customer or client. It could be about the process of developing and delivering the product and service. The job could provide an important sense of self-esteem and self-worth; it could be a mix of all these factors and more. The development of your workforce plan is about you and your business; however, it is also bigger than you. The work your employees perform is also about them, their dreams, and aspirations; it's a big deal.

> ***And whatsoever ye do, do it heartily as to the Lord***
> ***and not unto men*** – Colossians 3:23 (KJV)

Activity 1: Employment Reflection

Take a moment to write what you would like employment with your organization to mean to your organization, you, and your employees.

I would like for employment at my organization to _____

_____

_____

_____

The next step is to identify the positions needed to successfully run your business. Here you will need to step *inside and outside* of your business and imagine yourself as a customer and client. Take a moment to also imagine that you are a supplier and vendor. Imagine yourself as a citizen and creditor. What should these stakeholders see or what will they expect? What positions will be needed to meet those expectations? For example, our pizza store owner will need two cashiers, two cooks, and one driver. Now, of course, the immediate need for those positions may not occur for quite some time; yet, the planning for that position is part of our initial start-up strategy. Let's place your workforce planning in the context of the overarching business strategy.

Activity : Identifying Job Families and Positions

Take a moment to identify the job families that you think your company will need within the next five years. Write those positions below (Note: To ensure you can get your "arms" around this task, please do not exceed five positions for now).

Position 1:

Position 2:

Position 3:

Position 4:

Position 5:

Here it's important to recognize that these positions serve as the foundation for your initial job family. Now with these positions identified, you can outline the bundle of skills, knowledge, and abilities needed to perform in these roles and/or the behaviors and competencies you need your employees to have. Yet, before you get into this, I want to bring forward that many business development leaders and consultants go with the line of thought that you list the minimum qualifications. Believe it or not, I am not going to recommend such an approach. There are a couple of reasons why this is the case. First, you do not even have a baseline of performance to which to start such a process. Some explanation is in order. If you were scientifically developing your workforce plan, you may use references such as the Directory of Occupational Titles. This source provides standard job descriptions and baseline data that serve as a source to shape a business's workforce requirements. The unique requirements are then later addressed to fit the specific needs of the company. Again, that is the theory. However, because businesses are so unique, you are going to take a different approach. You are going to employ an approach that focuses on the things that are at the forefront of the business owner and leader's minds – your mind: how can I define my positional requirements that promote innovation, efficiency, and effectively engage employees? How can I define my positions, and in a manner that engages the employee and ensures critical tasks are being performed that contribute to customer satisfaction and loyalty? What's included herein is a process that helps you to reach these considerations, while at the same time allows you the room to develop an approach that meets your company's specific needs.

Having said this, you do not need to "throw the baby out with the bath water." It's important to recognize the utility of the approach I described above. One of the benefits to the approach is that it helps develop an efficient mindset. That one of the important objectives in hiring is to list staff requirements efficiently and effectively to achieve a positional fit. The drawback is that it remains largely skewed to an industrialist philosophy that does not effectively consider the needs of the contemporary business – your business. Having written this, you do need to think about these elements as you develop underlying policies and operational-based hiring plans, but for now, we want you to think of the bundle of attributes (knowledge, skills, abilities, behaviors, and competencies) needed to successfully deliver on our company's value proposition, and to meet its aims and objectives. So let's get started.

Activity 3: Knowing the Work

Position 1:

Knowledge

Skills

Abilities

Behaviors

Competencies

Position 2:

Knowledge

Skills

Abilities

Behaviors

Competencies

Position 3:

Knowledge

Skills

Abilities

Behaviors

Competencies

Position 4:

Knowledge

Skills

Abilities

Behaviors

Competencies

Position 5:

Knowledge

Skills

Abilities

Behaviors

Competencies

Now having these initial job factors identified, you need to take a moment to identify how that job looks in motion.

Position 1:

Job Duties and Tasks:

_____

_____

_____

_____

_____

Position 2:

Job Duties and Tasks:

_____

_____

_____

_____

_____

_____

Position 3:

Job Duties and Tasks:

_____

_____

_____

_____

_____

Position 4:

Job Duties and Tasks:

_____

_____

_____

_____

_____

Position 5:

Job Duties and Tasks:

_____

_____

_____

_____

_____

_____

Take a moment to review your work. A lot of ground was covered, and you likely see how firm your human capital roadmap is starting to take shape. Logically thinking, the next step is to come up with a means to evaluate the factors needed to perform the job and how the job is designed, a form of a job evaluation. Those of you that may have had a job prior to launching your business may remember those days when we you were interviewed, observed, and in some cases, even recorded to gain some insight into how work is performed within the organization. You need to take a similar approach. The reason is because your job positions and the tasks inherent within those jobs are not going to be static. The environment in which your organization works is dynamic, the response from your competitors is going to be dynamic, and the general business landscape will change.

With this in mind, we have a twofold objective. The first objective is to identify the methods of how you are going to evaluate the positions. The second objective is to develop an initial schedule to recruit to the position Let's start with the first task. There are several ways that you may evaluate the work performed by you and your employees. Common methods include interviews, actual performance of the job, observations, and questionnaires, which are the most popular methods. All these methods have their advantages and disadvantages. Further, these methods work well when resources and time permits and are often used in combination. For now, take a moment to reflect on your business and its needs.

Activity 4 – Evaluation Method Tools

Take a moment to circle one-to-two job evaluation methods that you think are suitable for business.

Interviews   Questionnaires   Performing the Job Yourself

Observation Performance of Employee

Next, please take a moment to outline the rationale of why you selected these methods:

_____

_____

_____

_____

_____

Important as the evaluations are, equally important is the scheduling of the evaluation. As your business matures, you will gain some idea on how often the job evaluation needs to be scheduled. For now, I recommend that you schedule the job evaluation on an annual basis.

Now that you have taken care of what is commonly referred to as the "space" of your position, now it's time to talk about the "face." The first activity is to come up with projected hire dates and identifying any barriers to you being able to fill your position requirement. Let's get to it.

Activity 5 – Filling the Space

Position 1:

Projected Need:

Barriers to Fill:

Position 2:

Projected Need:

Barrier to Fill:

Position 3:

Projected Need:

Barrier to Fill:

Position 4:

Projected Need:

Barrier to Fill:

Position 5:

Projected Need:

Barrier to Fill:

Next you need to identify where this talent is located, your labor market. When considering this task, think about all the possible places where your talent may be located. You may have talent in the area (city and state). You may have to reach across the country, or even across the globe. Take a moment to review your positional requirements and how the job is designed, and think about where the source of talent resides and how much that talent costs. Let's get started on our remaining two activities.

Activity 6: - Locating, Costing, and Reaching Talent

Position 1:

The location of talent is in the following areas (city, state, country) (Suggested sources of information may include city and county government websites, local chamber of commerce, and Department of Labor websites):

_____

_____

_____

Cost of Talent (Willing/Able to Pay) (Suggested sources of information may include city and county government websites, local chamber of commerce, and Department of Labor):_____

Means to Reach (Social Media, Internet Job Postings, Professional Associations/Networking): _____

Cost to Reach _____

Position 2:

The location of talent is in the following areas (city, state, country) Suggested sources of information may include city and county government websites, local chamber of commerce, and Department of Labor websites): _____

Cost of Talent (Willing/Able to Pay) (Suggested sources of information may include city and county government websites, local chamber of commerce, and Department of Labor):_____

Means to Reach (Social Media, Internet Job Postings, Professional Associations/Networking): _____

Cost to Reach _____

Position 3:

The location of talent is in the following areas (city, state, country) (Suggested sources of information may include city and county government websites, local chamber of commerce, and Department of Labor websites): _____

Cost of Talent (Willing/Able to Pay) (Suggested sources of information may include city and county government websites, local chamber of commerce, and Department of Labor):_____

Means to Reach (Social Media, Internet Job Postings, Professional Associations/Networking): _____

Cost to Reach _____

Position 4:

The location of talent is in the following areas (city, state, country) (Suggested sources of information may include city and county government websites, local chamber of commerce, and Department of Labor websites): _____

Cost of Talent (Willing/Able to Pay) (Suggested sources of information may include city and county government websites, local chamber of commerce, and Department of Labor):_____

Means to Reach (Social Media, Internet Job Postings, Professional Associations/Networking): _____

Cost to Reach _____

Position 5:

The location of talent is in the following areas (city, state, country) (Suggested sources of information may include city and county government websites, local chamber of commerce, and Department of Labor websites): _____

Cost of Talent (Willing/Able to Pay) (Suggested sources of information may include city and county government websites, local chamber of commerce, and Department of Labor):_____

Means to Reach (Social Media, Internet Job Postings, Professional Associations/Networking): _____

Cost to Reach _____

Total HR Process Costs:

Summary

Within this section, you completed many activities – you have developed a comprehensive plan to address what is (or will be) your most important resource – your employees. Specifically, you defined how working in your company will provide meaning to employees. Your employees will work for your company for several reasons. Some of these reasons will be explicitly stated, while others may go untold. In both cases, your work is important to you and your company, as well as your employee. You revisited and developed positions needed to deliver on your company's value proposition and critical to achieving its goals and objectives. Next, you captured the essential bundle of skills, knowledge, abilities, behaviors, and competencies and followed this with how the job is designed and evaluated. You closed out by focusing on getting the actual *body* in the job, focusing on when you need the employee and the barriers that you face in filling your job requirements. You did a lot, and you should be proud that you developed your initial human resource strategy.

CHAPTER 9

Identifying and Leveraging Technology

And the LORD said, Behold, the people [is] one, and they have all one language; and this they begin to do: and now nothing will be restrained from them, which they have imagined to do – Genesis 11:6 (KJV)

From the very beginning, your business is collecting information and intelligence. This information, in today's world, is ideally collected using technology. Just about every entrepreneur that I speak with has an idea of how she wants to employ technology. Yet, when I ask for a technology strategy that supports and aligns with the business strategy, rarely is one in existence – and that is a problem. Technology is a key enabler of business strategy, whether you are large or small, and to not have a technology business strategy plan results in you not having a key element that is important to business success.

Now when I ask about the lack of having a technology business strategy, generally, the answer falls along the lines of "Why do we need a technology strategy, we are a real estate investment group," or "It's too early for a technology strategy; we do use social media and the internet, and we know how we want to use it." These and similar answers generally fall short of what it really means and just how valuable having a technology strategy is to your business. Take for example a small-start-up consulting company. The company has five permanent employees and hires, on average, fifteen – twenty contractors. Between its marketing activities, bidding processes, accounting/financing activities, and software programs, it is not unreasonable to think that the company can operate with ten-plus software programs across various platforms, all essential to its business success. No matter your business, there is a form of technology. From the invoice that you use to confirm receipt of goods, to the software you use to collaborate with team members – and you need a technology strategy. In short, your business records and acts on information, and having a business technology strategy that captures how you will employ intelligence, systems, and information is critical to your business success.

Now, there is a debate on the role of technology in business and that is a point that we are going to address. In corporate speak, the argument seeks to determine if technology is a driver of your business or an enabler of your business. Some of the points of the debate are applicable to your business; yet, before you even think about entering such debates, you need to go about the process of discovering the role and impact of technology on your business. For our purposes, **technology** is inclusive of information technology and systems as well as manual processes, diagrams, workflows, and other processes that collect, store, record, and disseminate information in the course of delivering its products and services.

Let's get started.

Activity 1: Defining Technology Value and Processes

You need to know the role of technology in your business. To do this, you need to identify where and how you use technology and the value it has to your business. In considering the technology definition above, take a moment to outline how your business uses technology in the following areas:

Achieving Cost Savings/Gaining Efficiencies:

_____

_____

_____

_____

_____

Product/Service Introduction:

_____

_____

_____

Product/Service Improvement:

_____

_____

_____

Marketing:

_____

_____

_____

Supplier- Distributor Collaboration:

_____

_____

Professional Services:

_____

_____

_____

Customer Support:

_____

_____

_____

Finances and Accounting:

_____

_____

_____

Managing Talent:

_____

_____

_____

Activity 2: Current Technology Mediums

Next, you need to capture the current technology mediums and the processes that these mediums support. In conducting this exercise, please reflect on the technology definition above. While capturing these mediums, think about how your business currently uses technology. Take a moment to capture the current mediums and pieces within the medium that you employ within your business. A medium can be an invoice binder, notebook, or computer. A piece within the medium can include customer information, a specific software program, or receipts.

Current technology mediums include:

_____

_____

_____

Current technology pieces include:

_____

_____

_____

Activity 3: Identifying Redundancies

When you think about the true value of technology, the first thing that may come to your mind is efficiency and effectiveness. Whether it's a simple software program, or a complex collaboration platform, the true value of technology is that it saves time and enhances the ability to get things done. Yet too often, business owners complicate technology by having redundant files or conflicting information within documents. Think of something as simple as opening your first set of books: You bought the software, set up your balance sheet, income statement, and cash flow statements. The invoice register was then setup, and your clerk was tasked to use it – and in fact, he can use it better than you. Yet when you get rushed, you get out an old invoice pad that you keep. You use pen-and-pad, because you are comfortable with the old way of doing things, to record the delivery of goods and services that will later have to be put back into your accounting software. Of course, it does. Yet, I see business after businesses that employ redundant processes and workflow.

Of course, not much thought is put in to it. Yet when you start to scale, you will really feel the impact of having multiple processes for a single task or purpose, or having redundant data stored in different systems. In order to avoid all that drama, you will start, right now, to think about how you can reduce redundancies.

Think about some important office and general administration processes that your business performs. From the moment you buy supplies and material, to the process of transforming input to products, to the actual delivery of your products and services to the market. Also think about the efforts you put into marketing and sales and getting your product or services to the point of exchange (your restaurant, your store, your business, your car lot, etc.). Having this in mind, take a moment to think about where you store the following categories of information and the cost of the system (estimated). The sources of information may be software systems, programs, or manual technology sources like notebooks and shoeboxes. Take a moment to write down these sources:

Customer Information (estimated cost of system/software):

_____

_____

_____

Supplier Information (estimated cost of system/software):

_____

_____

_____

Finance/Accounting Information (estimated cost of system/software):

_____

_____

_____

Operations and Policy Information (estimated cost of system/software):

_____

_____

_____

Marketing Information (estimated cost of system/software):

_____

_____

_____

Employee Information (estimated cost of system/software):

_____

_____

_____

The next task within these activities is to find ways that you can streamline your data and the technology that records your data. Take a moment to think about ways that you can centralize your data and record your thoughts below:

_____

_____

_____

_____

_____

_____

Next, let's define the technology (systems or software) that will enable you to (a) centralize data; (b) retrieve data to where it's needed in all core business processes mentioned above; and (c) record the information in as few steps as possible. Take a moment to do that now:

_____

_____

_____

_____

_____

_____

The final step is finalizing your system, software, and manual technology list. Take a moment to think once again about your business *soup-to-nuts* and write-down the systems, software, and manual technology list that you must have to meet your business needs (Note: This list should be shorter than what you started with in the beginning of this activity. Please do not confuse it with a wish list.)

_____

_____

_____

_____

_____

_____

Activity 4: Technology and Your Business

Take a moment to reflect on what you just accomplished. Do you feel good? You should because you've essentially set-up your initial IT architecture – and you did it considering an inclusive definition of technology. Make no mistakes, it will grow and change, but for now, you should be proud of the work you've accomplished in this section. However, you are not done yet. Remember that discussion that outlined the debate of whether or not technology was a driver or an enabler? Well, you have a chance to at least start the discussion as it pertains to your business. And believe me when I say this: this is not merely just an administrative exercise. Your view will matter from the moment you write this statement and throughout your business lifecycle. So let's get to it. The last activity is for you to reflect on what technology means for you and your business – what purposes does technology serve. Take a moment to reflect and write that reflection below:

_____

_____

_____

Summary

Within this section, you defined the value of technology and technology processes to your business. Next, you identified specific technology mediums in your business that are currently employed to deliver value to your customer and clients to improve efficiencies. This was followed by identifying redundancies within your current technology processes that impact the efficiency or quality of your business. This chapter ended with a reflection on the role of technology within your business. You have done a great deal of work within this section, and you should be proud because you have essentially set-up an initial (or started the groundwork for an improved) IT business architecture. How you think about the role of technology is not only important for your business strategies, it helps create an awareness of how technology can be employed to make your business better.

CHAPTER 10

Standing Guard

He is like a man which built an house, and digged deep, and laid the foundation on a rock: and when a flood arose, the stream beat vehemently upon that house, and could not shake it: for it was founded upon a rock – Luke 6:48 (KJV)

There are elements of your business that will distinguish you in the marketplace. Now, I noted above how human capital, people (your employees and key partners), are the source of any sustained competitive advantage. As important as your talent is going to be in enabling you to achieve any sustained advantage, also important are the knowledge, information, products, and processes that signal to your customers, *here is where we are different*. We addressed much of the systematic approach to how this helps shape your long-term and short-term objectives. Here, you will take some time to consider the ways you can protect inventions, information, ideas, technologies, systems, and processes.

A theme that can be discerned in the biblical verse above is the importance of having a foundation and protecting that foundation. Let me reiterate a couple of points that we covered so far. When you entered the marketplace, there was likely some notice by someone that may be classified as a competitor. Next, for many of you, your product addresses or defines a unique need. Now, as was also previously, discussed, there are people that will address the need as well – no matter how unique you think the invention and need. Together, these serve as reasons for you to stand guard, to protect, to the best of your ability, the elements of your business that make it unique.

Permit me some space to talk about this for a second to put this in some sort of perspective. What I see in the early stages of business formation is an obsession to overprotect. This generally disguises inaction on the part of business owners and leaders. To patent and trademark everything seems like activity. I mean it's not picking up the phone or making sales calls. It's not giving presentations or traveling to trade shows, but it feels like activity. So, as business planning continues, the perception that a tagline or process is unique signals, *let's trademark this tagline*, or *patent that process* without any real tangible need or proof that doing so is worth the effort, thereby creating costs with no real action being taken to generate revenue. Essentially, the company has an idea for a product, service, and a bunch of trademarked taglines and patented systems.

On the other end of the spectrum are companies that are not vigilant enough. These are the companies that view the cost as unnecessary and burdensome. I see this quite often in entrepreneurs that believe that (a) the costs of acquiring and maintaining a patent does not provide the necessary level of protection and benefits; and, (b) that *patent watchers* will make the necessary minor adjustments that makes the patent essentially non-enforceable.

Let me cut right to the chase of the debate: protecting your business ideas, processes, technologies, and inventions is important and necessary; yet rarely, is it sufficient. When you have your ideas compromised, borrowed, or used without your permission or consent, it is painful. Many of you have already had this happen to you. In fact, I too was pained when I saw a whole work printed almost completely wholesale within a book without my knowledge or consent. What made this painful is that the work was shared among a group of peers and a college instructor, who maintained our works. It was one of the most jarring events that happened to me, so I know the importance of protecting intellectual property and other *intangibles* that provide your business with some advantage or distinction. Part of standing guard is to know what to protect, when to protect it, and how to protect it. We are going to cover these areas. Before we get into activities that will establish a framework, let's get the concepts and differences in order.

Activity 1: Worth the Protection

Take a moment to assess your intellectual property, processes, phrases/taglines, technologies, systems, or other inventions that make your business product or service unique. List intellectual property that you think warrants consideration for a patent or trademark.

Property: _____

Processes: _____

Phrases/Taglines: _____

Technologies: _____

Methods/Other: _____

Activity 2: Worth the Weight

Of the areas you listed above, please rank the top three items (Note: Three items is not required, you may only have one item listed. Some of you in a true commodity may not have any at this point in your company's lifecycle). Assign a weight between one and nine. When ranking, please consider the value to your business. Ask yourself, *does the asset create considerable value that can be reasonably protected? Is the asset truly unique and would it impact your business to maintain its distinction in the marketplace? Will you license, sale, or later lease the asset? Is this a significant consideration for investors to consider? Will it have a significant impact on your company's ability to raise capital?* Based on these and other considerations you deem important, please rank your top three (if applicable):

(1) _____

(2) _____

(3) _____

Activity 3: Worth the Investment

Please take a moment to write down the estimated cost of protecting your assets and the projected gains from the assets in the blanks below. Follow this by a rational statement that you can later refer to as you and your team has the benefit of reflection. An example of an estimated cost continuing with our pizza example, may be a deep oven, which may be $2,200. The projected payback for the over would be total gross sales of the pizzas cooked within the oven.

Estimated Cost (1): _____

Projected Payback: _____ (3 – 5 Years)

Estimated Cost (2): _____

Projected Payback: _____ (3 – 5 Years)

Estimated Cost (3): _____

Projected Payback: _____ (3 – 5 Years)

Total Estimated Cost: _____

Total Estimated Benefit: _____

Bonus Checklist

Filing patents can be a time-consuming and expensive process. We wanted to take a moment to provide you with some information and guidelines when considering a patent.

The United States Patent and Trademark Office (USPTO) classify three categories of patents. The three patent classification categories are *utility*, *design*, and *plant*. The general elements that you should consider, as outlined by the USPTO are as follows:

Novelty: In simple terms, this means that the invention must be unique. The invention could not have been made previously available in the public or within the public domain.

Usefulness: The invention must provide some utility. The USPTO has the specific definitions for each category listed above, bringing forth the requirements for the invention to be considered within each classification area.

Non-Obviousness: In simple terms, it requires that the invention provide impact. What I tell entrepreneurs that I consult with is that ensure your invention means something.

Additional information on patents can be obtained from the United States Patent and Trademark Office (see below) and from the source below.

Resources and References

The Law of Patents. (2008). *ASHE Higher Education Report, 34*(4), 53-76.

United States Patent and Trademark Office. Visit http://www.uspto.gov/web/patents/howtopat.htm

A talebearer revealeth secrets: but he that is of a faithful spirit concealeth the matter – Proverbs 11:13 (KJV)

Closely related to patents and trademarks is the notion to protect areas of your business that provide it with some distinctive advantage in the marketplace. Trade secrets fall under this category. For our purposes, a **trade secret** is information that is instrumental to developing processes, creating knowledge, or developing systems that provide measurable value to your business. A quick way to think about this is that if the information significantly contributes to your company's ability to achieve a competitive advantage, there is a high likelihood that it is a trade secret. Think of the pizza owner, discussed earlier. If there is a unique recipe that makes the pizza unique from competitors, this would be considered a trade secret just as KFC original recipe is considered a trade secret. What it means for you as an entrepreneur and business owner is that you should take measures to protect your trade secrets.

This may work against your spiritual nature, which may be to trust others; yet, we will be naïve to think that there are not talebearers or gossips among us. Having written this, take a moment to reflect on the information that is important to your business being able to become and remain distinctive and unique in the eyes of your customers and clients. What measures are you taking to safeguard information against disclosure to a dishonest person? What measures do you need to implement?

Protecting your trade secrets is no trivial matter. It is very important to your strategic success. Companies such as Intel, Apple, Microsoft, along with companies such as Chick-fil-A, McDonalds, and scores of consulting companies have trade secrets. It is an area of business that is not discussed enough. I have seen too many entrepreneurs take years' worth of work and effort, only to find that their trade secrets were compromised. You are – or will soon be – in a world where information on and about your company will be shared among various parties. There are investors, banks, journalists, writers, customers, and suppliers that will be exposed to the nuances of your business; it is wise to take the necessary measures to protect yourself. And, it is not enough that you know how to protect them, but also, that your employees, partners, suppliers, managers know how to protect your company's information.

Some ways that you can protect your information is to password protect data, store information in safes, have off-site storage, and protect access to certain areas of your premises. This is a judgment call on your part, but it's important to put some thought into protecting your trade secrets. Some specific (and standard) ways of protecting your trade secrets is to have employees and potential investors sign non-disclosure statements (a practice that I often follow). Here is the deal: Those that provide you money will often scuff at the idea of signing any paperwork that holds them to secrecy when they see information like (or similar) to your information every day. It's just not practical to require of each investor. This is why the consideration of filing patents is so important. Protecting your intellectual property is not only important, it's strategic, which is why we are covering it.

Activity 4: Trade Secrets Protection – Means and Methods

Take a moment to write down the means and methods that you employ in protecting your trade secrets:

_____

_____

_____

_____

Take a moment to write down the means and methods that you think should be employed to protect your trade secrets:

_____

_____

_____

_____

Summary

In this section, there was a discussion on the role and value of intellectual and intangible property on your business strategy. Specifically, there was a discussion on the value that trademarks, patents, and trade secrets have on your business. These are strategic level considerations that are often missed in even the most comprehensive books on strategy. Your business, even if you are in a business that provides a commodity, is creating knowledge and developing processes every day. Whether you are looking ahead three to five years down the road or performing present-day activities related to your action plans, you are creating valuable knowledge and information, which is critical to your business. In reflecting deeply and going through these exercises, you now have a means to consider the strategic implications. You will need to ensure that this is covered and addressed in your policies, so that the managers and employees within your company can take reasonable safeguards and measures to protect your intellectual property.

CHAPTER 11
Setting the Foundation

*By this shall all know that ye are my disciples, if ye have love one to another-*John 13:35 (KJV)

With your spiritual foundation serving as the base, you have set (or reset) your business based on spiritual principles and values. In addition, you have developed a series of plans in key business areas, which will serve as your roadmap for the next few years. That's impressive; yet there remains much work to do. You may remember us talking about how your business is a piece of you, yet larger than you. The weight of that thought may have really hit home as you begin *getting your hands dirty* and developing your plans.

Your next step is for you to start thinking about establishing an infrastructure; to begin setting a foundation for how your business will coordinate activities and actions to provide value to society. To become itself an entity capable of sustaining a life independent of you. The key action now is for you to reflect on your business and decide how you want to design your infrastructure. There are several ways you can go about accomplishing this. Traditionally, many start-ups and business mature around functions (i.e. marketing, human resources, research and development, operations, manufacturing, etc.). These approaches work well hence their popularity continues; however, this is not the only approach. You may also consider designing your organization around the product, based on a project, or create cells of teams. You may employ a team with a mix of skills and expertise; a team t or remote team mix. This is something for you to think about, and there is no better time than now.

> ***But ye shall receive power, after that the Holy Ghost is come upon you: and ye shall be witnesses unto me both in Jerusalem, and in all Judaea, and in Samaria, and unto the uttermost part of the earth.*** – Acts 1:8 (KJV)

Activity 1 – Structure Reflection

Take a moment to reflect on how you envision the best way to structure your business. Please feel free to think beyond the traditional approach, while also recognizing the utility and value of incorporating elements associated with that approach. Let's get started:

I/We envision that our business is best served by a structure that _____

_____

_____

_____

Based on your reflection, which structure best describes your business (please circle one):

Product-Based   Team-Based   Project-Based   Matrix

Functional   Network   Remote

It is important to recognize that your business may contain elements of more than one structure. That is expected and recognized. However, for purposes here, you need to identify the primary structure of your company. Also important to mention is that you are not dogmatically tied to any structure. As you continue to learn based on feedback and reflection, as well as the actual growth of your company, you may make adjustments to your business structure.

Earlier in this section, it was mentioned that functional-based approaches were common in business. Your business may have a different primary structure; yet, that are process and practices that can be related to the functional-based approaches discussed in this section that you need to consider (Note: How you view functions may vary; however, you will have functions within your primary structure). My intentions here are to briefly describe the important functions and have you reflect and briefly record how this fits within your organizational structure.

Marketing: Creating awareness and maintaining customers/clients is something you are likely well aware of and many entrepreneurs, business owners, and leaders are naturals when it comes to the tactical execution of traditional marketing processes – remember the four p(s) of marketing: product, place, promotion, price. What I also find is that many entrepreneurs and business owners are very strong at promoting and building brands. Most that I meet are also very strong at product development, especially, if they are the founders. Pricing and placement, I find greater challenges – especially, when it comes to knowing margins and cost of making the product. In any case, you will need to think about all these elements. You will need to know what your brand stands for and how to build brand equity. You will also need to know how to manage your changes and how to create "push-pull" strategies that support the customer receiving the product where and when they need it and how they want it.

Human Capital Management: How you manage your people and teams is so important that we have a whole section dedicated to it (see **Chapter Four**). Yet, there are several other elements to consider. Human capital management consists of planning and developing how your employees are recruited, hired, trained, and compensated. This area of your business also includes how your business will enforce policies and laws, and design its benefits. Finally, you will need to think about how you will build healthy work environments so that your employees *check-in* and stay engaged.

Finance/Accounting: Here is another section that you spent some time developing in Chapter 6. Specifically, there was discussion on key accounting statements, and you took the time to develop initial estimates that you can feed into your final budget. It is my hope that you find this section useful and view it as important to your strategy planning efforts. You know, when talking to and visiting with clients, the areas that seem to provide the most confusion and causes the most stress are the company's accounting and finance processes. And, as you can imagine, this is a problem. Finance and accounting is much more than just about our financial statements – although to keep these current and accurate is a task in itself. It's about ensuring that your company makes smart capital investments. A sound financing and accounting process helps to determine the cost of company activities; provides insight into how the company generates returns on monetary assets, and provides, on-demand, average aging of receivables and payables. It is the function where you need to know your company numbers and not only know the numbers but use data output to gauge the operational health of your company.

Operations/Manufacturing: This is an area that if you are not passionate about, then you will need to become passionate about it, or find someone who will, while making yourself a diligent student. Not knowing the impact of run times, set-up times; not knowing the cost and impact of waste and defective products and services can literally put you out of business.

R&D/Innovation: With companies having increased insight and information, the ability to imitate processes and systems quickly is common. Thus even low-cost approaches are now requiring some form of innovation. Your ability to differentiate your product and services is continuous and ongoing. Here is where innovation and research and development (R&D) processes come into play. Your company may, at some point in time, need to be able to provide a new way to delivery an experience or product. It will be well-served by owning a niche within a niche. It's up to you and your team to think about how to do this.

Information Systems Management: This is another area that you spent some time developing. A key insight that you should have gained from your work is that IT costs can "sneak" up on your business and become quite expensive to maintain. In addition, not only can these costs become significant, the payback and return from your IT can become difficult to measure. Contributing to this is that many companies fail to measure the value of their IT systems while investing or developing duplicate systems and processes, which minimize the benefit tied to the task that the technology is designed to enhance. Your information systems and management infrastructure are designed to work for you and your company, and you have taken some key steps to ensure that it accomplishes these aims.

That's quite a bit to reflect on, and you will need to think about these functions; let's call them processes to make it more inclusive, which leads us to our next activity.

Activity 2 – Process Reflection

Please reflect on the above processes (formerly known to us as functions) and write down how these processes will be employed in your business. I held off on having you do these separately because I would like for you to take a system-based approach to viewing these processes. Please take a few moments to describe in detail how these processes look integrated into the fabric of your business. Make it rich and detailed – imagine that you are a tour guide as you walk a visitor through your company. Let's go.

My business runs efficiently by employing business processes including

_____

_____

_____

_____

_____

Summary

In this section, you focused on the structure of your business. Specifically, you assessed and evaluated your company's business structure. This was important because the business structure you assume will impact just how your products and services are developed and delivered to your customers. You also had an opportunity to assess your approach to traditional business functions. Good work! Let's proceed to our next section.

CHAPTER 12

Rules of the Road

Let all things be done decently and in order – 1 Corinthians 14:40 (KJV)

There are two statements made by business owners that alert me that they need help and/or they have not really figured out the difference between entrepreneurship and just having a glorified title (owner) and working as an employee. One is the statement, "We would still be in business had it not been for _____." The second statement is, "I live here (here being their business)." The first statement we addressed earlier, and hopefully, that statement will be in the background once your business is positioned for health. The second statement is what we are about to address right now.

Have you ever been irked by a national brand (i.e. a major fast food restaurant chain or retailer) when there is a disconnect in the experience promised versus the actual experience delivered? When we see these disparities, that experience can set us off – ultimately, impacting our future buying decisions. It is crucial for your business to develop rules of the road, policies that work to decrease disparity of performance, so that your business can deliver on expected experiences from your customers and clients. Oftentimes, you will only get one shot at this.

Polices serve many useful purposes, and the business literature tends to overcomplicate the value of policies. My aim is to keep it simple and straightforward. Some important reasons for policies include:

- Having some predictability and consistency in performing activities, tasks, and actions
- Provide your employees required performance standards
- To reduce time spent making routine, standard decisions
- Reduce variations in outcomes
- Institutionalize practices into the fabric of your business culture

It's really that simple. Don't let various notions confuse you – cluttered thoughts are a sign of an unclear mind. Now with this framework in place, you will need you to create some basic policies for your company (or revisit and revise your existing policies). At this point, you may be fretting or panicking just a little, but if you look back on your existing activities, much of the input required for your policies has started. My contribution to this task is to provide some basic guidelines for you to consider before you start this important task.

Policy Development Guidelines

- **Header: Overview-** Develop a section of your policies around the organizational infrastructure support of your company. If, for example, your business has a project-team based approach, outline how these teams will conduct business (15 pages maximum).
- **Header: Employee Conduct-** Develop a section of your policies that focuses on employee treatment. How co-workers, owners, and contractors/vendors will be treated within your business. Please ensure you address issues such as harassment, managing disruptive behaviors (late/no-shows, walkouts, arguments, and counseling sessions), and how the discipline process works (15 pages maximum).
- **Header: Business Operations-** Develop a section of your policies that focuses on the processes (think functions) that we discussed above. Bring forward elements of that plan to incorporate into

your existing plan or as stand-alone (your preference) (15 pages maximum).

- **Header: Emergency Preparedness-** Develop a section for acts of nature and forces beyond your company's control (snowstorms, tornadoes, hurricanes, severe rainstorms, etc.) (5 pages maximum).
- **Header: Ethics and Compliance-** Develop a section of your policies that outlines the role of ethics and compliance. Review your ethical statements and capture that into specific actions. Within these actions, include elements that include resolving grievances (compliance), speaking with your managers within your company, and conducting meetings with external stakeholders (5 pages maximum).

The intention here is not to overprescribe an approach. Instead, I want to provide you with some general guidelines. This is a section within our strategic planning series that I honestly struggled on whether or not to include as a section. The reason why is because of its emphasis on operations versus strategy. However, in considering the challenges that I see many entrepreneurs and business owners face, I decided it was appropriate. Upon reflection, it's important for drawing a line between strategy and operations within a young company, and hopefully, you are starting to recognize the distinction and importance. It's important and is an area that I see even mature companies. I want you, at the very least, to have some basic approaches to these issues that can really hurt a young company. As time goes on, your policies will grow. Important for now is for you to think about these issues and how your company will respond when these issues come up; and believe me, these issues will come up. With that rationale developed, let's go into our only activity for this section, which is a one-day activity.

Activity 1 (Part 1)

Please write then develop the first two sections of your policies (organizational infrastructure and employee relations/conduct) employing the headers (or similar) as they appear.

Activity (Part 2)

Please write and develop the remaining three sections of your policies (business operations, risk planning, emergency preparedness, and ethics and compliance) employing the headers (or similar) appearing above.

Summary

In this section, the sole focus was on developing or revising your policies. Provided for you was a template that covered some important general areas applicable to most companies. You reflected on these areas and ideally, shaped some policies relevant to you and your business. It is important to note that you should ensure that your policies comply with applicable laws and regulations. Your policies must meet compliance standards and requirements where applicable, and may even exceed these standards, especially in areas that are consistent with your personal and business spiritual and core beliefs and values, distinguishing your product and service offerings. We will now turn our focus on developing a means to measure the actions, tasks, and activities that you've spend so much time focusing on within this course. Your strategy as it relates to operations in the form of operations – your strategy executed.

CHAPTER 13

Measuring it All

But thou shalt have a perfect and just weight, a perfect and just measure shalt thou have: that thy days may be lengthened in the land which the LORD thy God giveth thee – Deuteronomy 25:15 (KJV)

You now have a comprehensive framework that serves as your strategic and operational structure. Your duty now is to execute your strategy and action plans. As much hard work as you put into developing your strategy plan, the hardest task is to execute the plan. There are several reasons for this, which include the complexities of operating within a dynamic environment, the challenges of leading and managing people, and the difficulty of managing finite resources. In addition, your company doesn't operate in a static environment. You may be losing customers, gaining customers, or become faced with new demands from your customers. Your company is gaining new capabilities and will encounter capability gaps. Your company's financial positioning and sources of capital will change. Investments will need to be made, and increased capacity will be needed to meet demand.

Yet, you can succeed in execution, and the roadmap you developed in this field book serves as a guide. Is your planning going to be perfect? By no means is your planning going to be perfect. You are going to get some things right, and some outcomes are going to be below your expectations. You should and will make changes along the way as a result of learning and feedback, occurring in real-time. Having a measurement system in place serves as your business thermostat; your measurement system reads the health of your company, assessing the result of your "plan in action" and alerting you to elements of your business that are meeting your standards or performing below expectations.

Some questions you want to ask yourself should include: *Where are we excelling? Where are we meeting expectations?* And, *Where are we not meeting expectations?* The answers to these questions need to be quantifiable and measurable. Your leadership and management team need to continually ask, *What are we measuring,* and, *What areas of the organization should the measures be implemented and focused?* How you should proceed is the focus of this section. Specifically, you will develop some common-sense measurements and controls that matter to you. As challenging as this process will be, there is some good news: many of your competitors are (a) either not measuring, or (b) they are measuring the wrong things. How important is this? The ability to measure the right things and respond accordingly may mean the difference between your business being able to survive or capitalize on new opportunities. Measurements help you stay attune to your business environment and to the needs of key stakeholders within that environment. Measuring is serious business.

So where should your measurement system focus? You want your measures to focus on external and internal factors that are relevant. In other words, you need to know what's going on outside and inside the doors of your company where it matters. Focusing on the outside, some areas that you want to focus on include your competitors, suppliers, industry, and community. You also want to focus on laws, societal and economic trends, and changes in technology. Internally, you will need to focus on your customers and employees. So, let's get started.

One type of measurement approach that you may need within your business is **scheduled monitoring**. Here you will look externally and internally to assess specific factors relevant to your business. Here, you may conduct a scheduled review of what your competitors are doing in the area, as well as changes and trends in your industry. You may also conduct scheduled reviews of internal areas of concerns, asking questions such as,

What is our business's quarterly performance? Or, *What were the concerns and requests of customers over the last three quarters?*

A second measurement approach that you may need within your business is **unscheduled monitoring**. Think of unscheduled monitoring as just wanting to know what's going on today. Most of us do this in some kind of way, rather we recognize (or call) it as such or not. For instance, as a business owner and manager, you may read business periodicals quite often. You may also read reports on what's going on in the IT and human capital industries. These are all forms of unscheduled monitoring. It can be a miniature literature review that lets you know what's going on in an informed and, at times, scientific way. Or, it can be an unannounced visit to one of your business units or stores.

A third measurement approach is an **emergent event**. This approach can result from an event that warrants your attention. Examples of this may include a recall on beef at your restaurant, which has impacted the sale of burgers, or a new computer coding language that makes your website incompatible with some end-user devices. An emergent approach consists of alerts or triggers that alert you to the factor that is impacting your company's performance. As an example and related to the previous example, you may be working to update your website; however, you are alerted to the changes in standards related to programming language. The measurement enables you to make the right investment in the right area so that your site is functional across various platforms.

A final measurement approach is called **execution monitoring**. Execution monitoring focuses on the progress of the functional processes outlined in this plan, as well as projects and programs you developed that help facilitate you to achieve your business strategy. It is an approach to monitoring that links long-term planning with concrete action steps. Some of you may already have these in your companies. Examples of these include project plans or measurements such as the balanced scorecard system or key performance organization.

Now having an example of the various forms of measures, we will turn our attention to implementation and scheduled monitoring that aligns with the strategy you have developed. More specifically, we will develop measures that you can use, right now, in your business. For implementation and scheduled monitoring, sources of measurement may include your financials. Under this report type, you may have your accounts receivable (aging) report, accounts payable (aging) report, and financial statements. This can also include your project plans, your safety incident reports, systems uptime/downtime reports, and customer feedback surveys.

Activity 1 – Measurement Selection

Take a moment to focus on measurement selection. The types of measurements seem endless, and we recognize that. For now, reflect on some common measurements. Below are some of these measurements. Please review and identify those that are relevant to your business. Circle at least two measures per category that are relevant to your business. As you reflect on these, work to develop more specific and additional measures.

Financial Measures

Cash Flow/Income Statements   Return on Capital Report

Accounts Receivable   Accounts Payable

Client/Customer Measures

Market Share Reports   Customer Surveys

Share of Segment   Number of Repeat Customers

Operations

Safety Incident Reports   New Product Development Time

Capacity Utilization Report   Deficiency/Waste Reports

Workforce Measures

Turnover Reports (Voluntary/Involuntary)   Time to Fill Vacancy

Promotion Rate   Engagement/Employee Survey (Score)

Now that we have this developed, take a moment to reflect on and define why these measures are important to you.

My business financial measures are important to my business because

_____

_____

_____

My business client/customer measures are important to my business because

_____

_____

_____

My business operations measures are important to my business because

_____

_____

_____

My business workforce measures are important to my business because

_____

_____

_____

Activity 2 – Developing Targets

Targets are the actual performance we are trying to achieve. As an example, you may have a store sales target of $50,000 gross per month. Your actual performance may be $45,000 gross per month. So in this simple example, your operational-based target of growth for the month is $5,000 or 90% of the planned target. The question you may have at this point is what are appropriate targets? To that I say, *it depends*. Developing your initial targets is both an art and science in the early stages of your company; however, there are some standards of performance that can be baselined determined by industry performance standards. If you are just starting out, there are a couple of sources for information that you may use. This includes professional association data, industry reports, chamber of commerce information, available competitor information, and peer-review literature/reports. I recommend that you review three to five sources of information to help you in developing a baseline target and ensure that you have reasonable access to the sources. Please take a moment to identify three to five sources of information to help you baseline your data.

_____ _____ _____

_____ _____

Our next step is to review these sources and come up with some specific targets. Let's do that now (Note: This will likely shift as you review more information and gain experience. These are only baseline standards of performance. I have found that becoming familiar with the process of baselining, and actually doing it, facilitates action in the future).

Based on your selection above, please take a moment to establish a target that you think adequately defines success for your company. (Note: Not all measurements are necessarily quantitative; however; the above quantitative measures were intentionally established to help you set quantitative baselines. You likely will, and should consider qualitative data as well. For now, we need to baseline performance along a few key performance dimensions that are important to you and your business.

Please identify your measure (**first column**). In the **second column**, you will identify a strategic performance objective based on your research above. Next, you will set up the *Performance Period Goal/Period*. How you set-up your *Performance Goal/Period* is completely up to you; however, I do recommend that you apply rigor to the performance dimensions that align with the elements of differentiation or product/service distinguishers that you identified within the planning section. Next, you will also select a period, and record both elements in the **third column**. The initial period may change as it matures out. Over time, you will be able to make a decision on rather, or not to shorten or extend your initial performance period. The *Actual Performance* and *Performance Deviation* (**fourth** and **fifth columns** respectively) columns will be recorded after the initial observed performance period. Finally, you will take a moment to reflect, investigate, and assess the performance. Record these results within the *Comment* column. Below is a sample entry that can assist you.

Measurement	Strategic Performance Objective	Performance Period Goal/Period	Actual Performance	Performance Deviation	Comments
Stock Availability	Availability above industry norm and above that of competitors	95% in stock	90% in stock	5%	Under-estimated seasonal demand

Summary

In this chapter, there was a discussion on the four types of measurement approaches that include scheduled monitoring, unscheduled monitoring, emergent event, and execution monitoring. Next, you considered some current reports and thought about planned reports that would adequately capture value-added areas that are important to your business and developed (or revised) some key measurements. From there, you took time to develop targets within the key measurements listed in this section. You had an opportunity to evaluate, assess, and reflect on the role of measurement to your business. These measures were carefully selected and defined, and were based on the key strategic dimensions of performance, consistent with your strategic planning and execution. Finally, you completed an abbreviated performance management scorecard and summary report that can be incorporated and built-up going forward. Your next step is to capture a spirit of learning and sharing in your business, which will inspire everyone that comes in contact with your company to do the same.

CHAPTER 14

Developing and Implementing a Learning Environment

Beware lest any man spoil you through philosophy and vain deceit, after the tradition of men, after the rudiments of the world, and not after Christ – Colossians 2:8 (KJV)

From the moment you open your doors, your organization begins its lifecycle. Your business exists among an ecosystem of other businesses and will advance along its lifecycle based largely in part on its ability to adapt and respond to the dynamic forces and pressures that include, yet extend beyond, your customer. An area where you want to dedicate some thought to is just how you and your company nurture the spirit of learning.

One of the most important contributions made to the literary and conceptual world of business is by Peter Senge. Senge's *The Fifth Discipline* expanded on the notion of a learning organization. Without getting too theoretical, the learning organization is based on the premise that the organization interacts with its environment. Based on this interaction, over time, the organization acquires knowledge and responds to forces and pressures based on the knowledge it has acquired and its ability to employ the knowledge to its benefit. Additionally, your company's ability to survive will also depend largely on its *openness* to feedback and being able to honestly assess its purpose. Consistent with the theory is that a company will develop a systems perspective and see beyond isolated events and leverage leveraging insight gained from themes and patterns within its environment. This systems-based perspective considers the internal design of the organization and its role and place in the environment. It recognizes the importance of events, yet does not limit itself to an event-based view and is keenly aware of the gradual and emergent changes that can impact purpose, intent, and essentially, performance. At its most efficient and highest level, the company recognizes the drivers of change and how these drivers contribute to events. A true embracing of the concept can contribute to a company's ability to generate knowledge, employ knowledge, embrace learning, and foster cooperation.

The underlying premise has a spiritual dimension as well, and I find this is one of the few theoretical constructs that can fit our spiritually-based strategic planning and execution the best. You, your employees, and other key stakeholders will be well-served to recognize how your company works within a larger ecosystem. You should work to recognize how your organization's interaction with its environment impacts its structure and how these interactions may help you discover problems that may otherwise be misdiagnosed, if diagnosed at all.

For purposes here, a key strategic value is the emphasis on bringing forth the role of knowledge and learning at all levels. You can promote learning in various ways, which include finding efficient and effective means for your company to interact with its stakeholders and to increase its ability to understand internal competing demands, which impair performance. It also includes promoting and gaining the use of your customer and supplier voices. Hearing these various voices and implementing changes based on feedback will cause you to more efficiently partner with suppliers and deliver products or services in a better way to your customers that will lead to impact felt by you and your customer. It's promotes interaction with your customer by learning how they perceive product and service quality. Finally, a learning organization promotes and leverages its employee's voice. We've consistently covered the value of employees, and how considering their unique needs can provide value to you and your company.

You know this, and you went over several ways on how to take into account employee value in the human capital section. However, it bears repeating that some of the most important insights and knowledge will come right from your own employees. Your employees, in many cases, have invested a sense of who they are and their hopes and dreams into the success of your business. Your willingness to trust and empower them may prove instrumental in building a company that delivers on your business purpose. All too often I see businesses where owners literally live out their lives in the lobbies, offices, or on the floor of their businesses not realizing, that for all they know, they cannot know more than a truly united collective; a collective group of engaged stakeholders – customers, suppliers, employees, community citizens, and investors.

Activity 1: Promoting the Learning Organization

Based on the information presented above, how can you promote a learning organization? Take a moment to consider the three core groups we've named and write down your thoughts.

I can promote a learning organization in partnership with my suppliers by

_____

_____

_____

I can promote a learning organization in partnership with my customers by

_____

_____

_____

I can promote a learning organization in partnership with my employees by

_____

_____

_____

****

Having worked and taught through elements of establishing and maintaining a learning organization over the years, I've noticed three core business activities in which learning organizations can facilitate effort. These three areas are what I call the *three I's of learning*: integration, innovation, and inspiration. The leverage point of the three I's comes by the learning organizations focus on crossing boundaries, working in teams, and recognizing the art and value of reflection. Let's take some time to enhance and expand on your reflection above within the next activity that considers this insight.

Activity 2: Achieving Integration, Innovation, and Inspiration

Take a moment to review your reflections above. Based on those reflections, create a comprehensive statement in which you will achieve integration, innovation, and inspiration.

I will achieve integration, innovation, and inspiration in considering how my company currently learns and will learn in the future. The specific means in which I will achieve the Three I's is through:

_____

_____

_____

_____

_____

_____

Summary

In this section, you reflected on the different ways that your company learns and leverages the insight from this learning to create a learning environment. Specifically, you reviewed concepts related to the learning organization and how knowledge creation, employee empowerment, and customer and supplier insight can create value for your organization. You developed a comprehensive statement that centered on customers, suppliers, and employees and followed this with a statement of how you can successfully integrate the Three I's of Integration, Innovation, and Inspiration to address the unique needs of your core stakeholders. In the next section, the role of leadership and what it means for your company is discussed.

CHAPTER 15

Walking in Faith, Leading with Conviction

It is not this way among you, but whoever wishes to become great among you shall be your servant – Matthew 20:26 (NASB)

Having reached this point, it can be said that you have conducted some very extensive and rigorous activities needed to build your business. You have done what many business owners ignore or shy away from – you have developed a comprehensive strategy. Going further, the few business owners that I've seen develop a strategy do so in a very loose way that lacks any serious rigor. Finally, and most importantly, you have done this based on spiritual values and principles.

Yet as important as the work you conducted thus far is, it means nothing without your leadership. It means nothing unless you have the faith and conviction that you can, and will build a great business based on spiritual principles and values. It is my belief, having gotten this far that you can. Some questions that may be lingering in your mind is, *What specific areas of leadership should I focus my attention on?* Most entrepreneurs that I meet are strong in specific leadership areas. For example, many can motivate their employees to reach new heights and dig deep within themselves. They are good at generating a following and in the early goings, generating excitement about their products and services.

With this acknowledgment comes some truth. One truth is that many business leaders are not used to being challenged or can rationally address many of the challenges of business. In addition, there are many business owners who let their egos get them in trouble and blind them to events, pressures, and forces that many observers see, often quite plainly. In fact, these forces and pressures may be so strong that they eventually place the business at-risk of failing. I've seen business owners that lose everything they worked so hard to build. I've seen the impact of business failures on the business owners, families, and the communities.

As difficult as the tasks and activities we performed are, there is not one, in my experience, that is more difficult than the role of leadership. Leadership, by far, is the greatest challenge. Herein is not a prescriptive way on how to lead, for it's been my experience that while there are general leadership principles, dimensions, attributes, and behaviors, leadership remains very personal, often contextual, and extremely difficult to execute for prolonged periods of time. Yet, it is the order that you signed up to do when you put the livelihood of others under your influence. It's what's required when you are called upon to balance competing demands. For some, it may be the very opportunity to lead that business that drew you to pursue business ownership.

Recognize the Calling – Understand the Purpose

There will be times when you will face great challenges in running your business. You may be faced with lawsuits, disgruntled employees, or unhappy customers. There will be times when misunderstandings develop between you and your key business partners, your lawyers, contractors, and accountants. There will be times when a new competitor, who you had no idea was on the horizon, emerges and gains significant market share. There may even be times when you are technically insolvent and are struggling to keep the doors open. It is during these times that your resiliency and your faith will be tested. It is here that your spiritual purpose and knowing the purpose of your business will be so important, which is why being truly connected to your calling, your purpose will serve to ground you, to guide you, and to sustain you. Very rarely is a journey worth pursuing absent of challenge; yet, it's also your calling and your personal and business purpose, which can serve to keep you going. After all, for many, it's the source for even starting the journey to begin with.

Developing and Pursuing Vision

There are countless studies on the behaviors of leaders. What's consistent throughout the literature (scientific and commentary) is the ability of the leader to develop and pursue a vision. Going deeper, the leader has the ability to get others to believe in the vision and take ownership for its accomplishment. This last part is perhaps what makes leaders truly unique from effective managers. To gain followership, one must know how to identify the intrinsic nature of others. Great leaders understand that followers need to recognize the value of their actions, from an individual and shared perspective. Now, when we look at this for a second, is this not what Jesus did. Is this not what great leaders did stretching as far back as David in the Bible to as recent as Pope John Paul II, Dr. Martin Luther King, Jr., and Mother Teresa? This insight is not new. It's one of the longest standing, time-tested principles of effective leadership. It's what opened up our chapter and threads throughout the text of this book.

Adding to this is the expectation of the leader that he/she not only effectively communicates an ideal future state, but also be able to develop and articulate concrete steps to pursue that vision. Your employees, rightfully so, are going to expect this of you. They are going to look to you for both reasoning and inspiration. Your employees are going to recognize the difference between plans and rhetoric, and they are going to want a little of both. In short, your leaders are going to want you to lead them to an ideal future state through the articulation and achievement of concrete goals and tasks. It's arguably one of your tallest tasks in being a leader, and you are up for it.

Service to Others

Arguably, one of the greatest challenges of those that consider themselves leaders is recognizing the difference between being a leader and a manager. Without getting into the circular debate, there is a difference between the two concepts, and one of the least understood elements related to leadership is being of service to others. Yet, as the below verse captures, this concept is also consistent throughout the leadership literature that a leader is to be of service to others. It is the very essence and foundation of much of our work thus far. There are various labels for this behavior. The tags range from *self-sacrificing* to *subordinating the needs of self*; yet, in essence, to be of service to others results in the leader creating the conditions for excellence and bringing out the best in others. Your employees are going to look to you for moral and psychological support. They are going to need the right tools to do their job. They are going to need you to stand tall when customers, suppliers, and vendors are pushing them in ways that run contrary to your business aims and what it stands for.

Being of service also means that you are aware of what employees may need, even when it is not articulated. It means being aware of an employee's emotional needs and providing an appropriate intervention. It means knowing what they need from a job perspective and what they need from a career perspective. These notions may be simple to state; however, they are harder to execute for it may require that, at times, you may not get what you want in order to ensure the employee gets what they need. Perhaps, one of the most important quotes comes from the leadership scholar Bernard Bass, who states that "[s]ocialized charismatic leaders are oriented to serving others. They develop shared goals with their followers and inspire the attainment of such goals" (as cited in *Transformational and Charismatic Leadership*, p. 188[7]).

To put it simply: Leaders serve.

As shown in the quote from Matthew 20:26, leaders are loyal servants. What does this look like in your business? It means serving your customers. It means providing them the service and products that they expect, and meeting or exceeding expectations. Being a leader means stepping forward when others need you. It means you to maintain an awareness of your role and how your actions and behaviors impact individuals and groups, while aligning with the goals of your business.

---

[7] Bass, Bernard. Transformational and Charismatic Leadership. page 188.

Perhaps, in all of this, one of the biggest challenges for many people that aspire to be strong leaders is that the need has to be continuously recognized and applauded. To refrain from standing-out and instead work to ensure that others do. There are many wise men that capture this, and one of the most important sayings is brought forth by Lao Tuz who states:

The wicked leader is he whom the people revile.

The good leader is he whom the people revere.

The great leader is he of who the people say, "We did it ourselves." Lao Tzu, D.533 BC

Reaching and Teaching

I will instruct thee and teach thee in the way which thou shalt go; I will guide thee with mine eye - Psalm 32:8 (KJV)

Related to the notion of leadership is the notion of teaching others. Indeed, part of serving others is teaching so that others can develop the necessary skills, build and expand on one's knowledge base, and enhance the performance of individuals and teams. Arguably, one of the greatest rewards that you will experience (and many of you are already experiencing) is to observe others develop their capacity to solve problems, originate ideas, and execute actions instrumental and important to your business. When this growth develops, you are better off, your business is better off, and most importantly, the people who work for you and buy from you benefit from your sharing of knowledge – and ideally, are better for it. In fact, part of building your culture is creating an environment that supports the acquisition, transfer, and sharing of knowledge. Your authentic belief in reaching and teaching will come through in your business performance, employee retention rates, and workplace climate. If it's there, you may be surprised at the sacrifices that your employees are willing to make on behalf of your business. I have seen employees forgo higher-paying jobs and jobs which, on the surface, provide more prestige because of the knowledge, training, and development they received from their employer.

There is additional utility in teaching others that are important to your business. When you provide knowledge to employees, for example, their confidence increases, and they become engaged in their work. Often accompanying this increase in confidence and assuming a culture that supports this knowledge sharing and acquisition accompanies this, a *space* is created, a space in which your employee feels empowered. This space of discretionary effort and empowerment often creates a *spillover* effect, enabling your employees to more effectively meet the needs of customers and business partners. This enhances their experiences and increases their enthusiasm for your business.

And it doesn't stop there. Over time, your organization increases its capacity. It increases its capacity to respond to problems, create new solutions, and solve problems *at the line*. When this level is reached, great things often happen. Your organization gains an ability to better control its destiny, and the positive increase in trust you gain from your employees impacts customer loyalty and satisfaction, which increases the level of community trust, and it goes on-and-on, having an impact on your business purpose – remember that. Take a moment to reflect and review it.

Ability and Willingness to Adapt

An effective leader knows when to adapt. Great leaders know that in pursuing a vision, barriers will be along the path, information will change, and external and internal events will influence how the vision is achieved. Leaders that are otherwise effective, often, remain dogmatic in pursuit of business aims or along a course of action that does not acknowledge the dynamic nature of the business environment. These otherwise good leaders become married to strategies that don't work, or are no longer relevant or applicable given the current circumstances. One of the worst things that you can do as a leader is hold your team to a strategy that is no longer working; to fail to adapt to the events, information, and reality of the new environment. While it is true that effective leaders provide a sense of where the organization needs to head and what it needs to accomplish, these leaders also know when to change and adapt to the circumstances surrounding them in their business.

Confident and Resilient

Wherefore, my beloved brethren, let every man be swift to hear, slow to speak, slow to wrath– James 1:19 (KJV)

It is not this way among you, but whoever wishes to become great among you shall be your servant – Matthew 20:26 (NASB)

Being a strong leader that is confident and resilient serves you and your company well. In fact, your confidence and resilience will continuously be stretched, tested, and tried. As mentioned earlier, remaining in business over time, and building a great company is hard – very hard, and your employees will look to you. They will look to you when times are good and when times are not so good, and in both cases, for guidance, confirmation, and support.

You will be required to stand tall when your ethics are challenged. Your ability to think and rationalize under pressure will be both observed and required during upheavals within your business industry or the communities in which your business is a part of. There will, on occasion, be conflict between your employees, customers, and business partners, and here your confidence will be required. There will be times when you look at your income statement and see that sales do not cover outstanding debt, and for a moment (I hope), you will have to navigate your business and team through the storm. Many of you will find your confidence tested when you have to make a round of layoffs. I remember some of my most trying times as an entrepreneur were when the phone was silent for prolonged periods of times – and these times seem to almost always occur after a fruitful season. Having a period of momentum, followed by a period of famine, will test your resiliency, and I can almost guarantee you that each of you will be faced with times like such as this.

Take a moment to reflect on the values that you took time to develop earlier at the beginning of this book. As hard as you worked to develop those values and as much buy-in as you try to gain, there will be times when these values clash with an employee's value system. Your courage will be tested when you try to build a culture that will last. Yet, despite the challenges and degree of difficulty, building an enduring culture is arguably one of your most important undertakings. Your resiliency and confidence will be required.

One of my favorite teaching events is when I teach communication and psychology-based courses of instruction. One subject or discussion that is almost guaranteed to take place during these sessions is the line between confidence and arrogance. It's often framed as assertiveness versus aggressiveness, but the points are similar: being confident should not be confused with being arrogant. In fact, the leaders that we come across are often confident and humble. They know how to project assurance during tough times, while listening to the voices of others and demonstrating high levels of emotional intelligence. These leaders know how to take risks without exposing employees and other key stakeholders to consequences deemed intolerable or excessive. These leaders know how to communicate urgency, without creating alarm.

Here is a sobering and important point. As much as you put into your business, your business does not completely define you. It is a large part of you, but it is certainly not all of you. In 2014, the great actor and comedian Robin Williams' suicide shocked the world. Now, I don't presume to know all of what Robin was going through – in fact, I know next-to nothing about him, but it is well-known that His mental state ebbed and flowed throughout his career. When his career was up, he was generally up. When his career was down, he was generally down. Many of us are the same way. I admit, when I am up, my mood is up; however, when I am down, I tend to dive into temporary bouts of frustration and occasional depression – that is until I reflect on all the great things God has done for me and that I am much more than my businesses. You need to remember God's love for you when your confidence is shaken or your resiliency is tested. You are going to have setbacks sometimes, but when you do, know that with these setbacks come victories – come moments of insight and lessons learned that will make you better as a person, as a servant, as a leader, and as a business owner. Please do not wrap yourself so much in your business that you cannot step outside of it and realize all that God has to offer. In fact, recognizing your greatness and what God has planned for you will make you a better person in all aspects. You will be able to see beyond cycles and withstand periods when the stars don't align. You will recognize that great challenges often comes right before you achieve moments of breakthrough.

Activity 1– Leadership Statement

You have covered a lot of the tenants of leadership and the role of culture, providing you with an opportunity to reflect on your personal leadership approach and style, and the type of culture you want to build. Please take a moment to write down a personal leadership statement that considers the tenants of leadership and culture discussed in this section. This statement should be both personalized to who you are and consistent with the organizational and personal statements you developed earlier. Try not to exceed half of a page.

_____

_____

_____

_____

_____

_____

Summary

Within this section, you reflected on what it means to you to serve others. You thought through your leadership approach in addressing your service approach, and you discovered the tenants most commonly associated with servant leadership. Next, you took a moment to reflect on how you serve specific groups, specifically your employees. Here you assessed how you lead by example and navigate your employees through prosperous and challenging times. You read on what it means to be an adaptable leader and how you maintain the faith and confidence of your employees, customers, and other key stakeholder groups. You related this to your personal and business value you developed earlier in the course. Finally, you reflected on the role of culture and how your leadership approach, resiliency, and commitment to your business vision and mission create an enduring culture. You closed by developing a personal leadership statement that considered all the major elements of this section.

EPILOGUE

Congratulations. You have completed building a business based on the Blessed Strategy framework. You have re-mapped, revisited, and redesigned your business based on spiritual principles. You have demonstrated courage by not only stating that you want a business based on spiritual values and principles, but by taking concrete actions to make this a reality.

Make no mistakes this was not an exercise in stamina. Through Blessed Strategy, you now have a comprehensive strategic business plan that rivals the most comprehensive strategies of any company, of any size. Yet, how would you feel if I told you that you were only at the beginning. Well, this is just that. A beginning; a start. You have "miles to go before you sleep," and one of your commitments needs to be to continue and learn.

During this journey, it is my hope that you have had sufficient opportunity to reflect. It is also my hope that you had an opportunity to evaluate deeply who you are as a business owner, strategist, and entrepreneur. Next, I pray that this comprehensive journey provided you an opportunity to think deeply about your business and its role; its role in providing goods and services, providing employment, and acting as a social citizen. I also pray that you had time to consider your business's role in nurturing and contributing to community growth. Finally, it is my wish that you have an opportunity to revisit what I feel is one of the most important roles that you have: that of a spiritual role model and leader. This will be, in my opinion, the true endearing and lasting elements of your legacy.

As you pursue your journey, please don't lose sight that the key differentiator of your strategy and business plan is that it's based on a comprehensive spiritually-based framework; it is truly a Blessed Strategy. The mission, vision, and values are spiritually-based. The long-term and short-term planning is spiritually-based. The alignment strategy and the deep dives into the role of traditional business practices are all spiritually-based, and that, my valued reader and business leader, is something to be excited about.

There is value in this approach that is inclusive of yet extends beyond profit. First, you should recognize that businesses are essentially about purpose, and in your case, that purpose is grounded spirituality. Second, customers, employees, and your business value partners will take note of your commitment to this purpose and how it underlies your business planning and execution. Third, the culture and movement of your business will be distinguishable.

So you may be asking yourself, *Can I really get ahead operating a spiritually-based business?* My answer: Absolutely. There are countless examples of spiritually-based leaders who lead and grow extremely profitable businesses. Indeed, from my perspective, it is the key to achieving long-term growth and value with a conscience and purpose. What I find particularly rewarding in working with spiritually-based leaders is that they are concerned with the long-term implications and impact of their business decisions. They pay attention to not only outcomes but processes – recognizing that not any role will do. And, it is in this area what some may consider ironic: their businesses are not only thriving, but are often top-performers in their industry or market. Attracting brand product and service loyalty are not uncommon among these leaders. You recognize these businesses when you see them. The owners stand tall and face adversity with courage and conviction. They do not shrink from their responsibilities or casually alter views and their role in society to match current trends. They are always learning, sharing, and serving, and in return, we buy and are committed not only to the business products and services, but also to their purpose.

Wonderful things can happen when people connect to a purpose, especially a spiritually-based purpose. Employees begin to understand their roles beyond positions and see your business as a citizen and how they contribute to the purpose of the business and to the health of their community. Your employees will recognize your commitment to them and in return, conduct themselves as someone that values their role within your company, and pass these feelings on to your company's customers. Your employees will also recognize your commitment to developing mastery and competence that makes everyone better off. Your employees will recognize your commitment to helping them reaching their full potential as employees, as well as individuals.

Your business value partners will recognize the commitment you have to the success of their businesses. They will see how you seek and leverage opportunities to not only enhance your business, but to enhance their businesses as well. They will become inspired by your commitment to your employees and customers, and how you view them not as detached entities, but as members of an extended business family. They will marvel at how you are able to develop relationships that results in a cohesive, comprehensive experience. Your business value partners will recognize that as you work to exemplify your company's profit, doing good is not at odds with it, but each are supportive of each other.

And this, my dear reader, is only the beginning. Have a Blessed Strategy.

****

FINAL THOUGHTS

Writing this book for you has been both rewarding for me as well. I have had an opportunity to revisit my purpose and how I view the role of my businesses related to society, groups, and individuals. This was probably one of the most exhausting, yet exhilarating endeavors that I have pursued. Yet, I know that my own learning, commitment level, and service endeavors are not complete.

I am looking forward to meeting many of you as I work to share this work with you to make significant, measurable changes in your businesses. It is my sincere hope that you have a renewed passion for your business. It is my hope that you have expanded upon the notion that your business exists for so much more than profit alone. Furthermore, I hope that our exercises, reflections, and the retooling of your business plan and strategy has encouraged you to think deeply about the connection between you, your business, your community, and society.

Finally, and most importantly, I hope that this work has rekindled a fire within you from a spiritual perspective - that your faith in yourself and your purpose is renewed. Your relationship with God, in my view, is the most important relationship that you have. Too long, we have bought into this notion that our spiritual and relationship with God is something to hold separate and apart from business. That's nonsense. And as I hope you have discovered, some of the best entrepreneurs and business leaders are spiritually-based leaders who have stood tall and acknowledged the role of

God and spirituality as paramount to the success of their business success. These leaders are to be applauded, and so are you.

Walk in faith and do great things.

From one entrepreneur to another with Love,

George

www.ingramcontent.com/pod-product-compliance
Lightning Source LLC
Chambersburg PA
CBHW032001190326
41520CB00007B/315